Leave The B

C000141644

Also by Richard Maun

My Boss is a Bastard
Surviving turmoil at work

Do you have a reasonable, competent, fair-minded and even-tempered boss? Congratulations! You need read no further.

Still with us? Your manager may be difficult, temperamental, even downright brutal, but for the sake of your career (and your sanity), you must achieve some kind of working relationship. That's where *My Boss is a Bastard* comes in.

Richard Maun dissects the personality types that make bad bosses and offers practical tips to help you survive everyday encounters with the monster in your office. Once you have recognised the raw animal nature lurking beneath that professional exterior, you'll be better equipped to escape unscathed from your next brush with the boss. You can rise above the office jungle and move towards a more fulfilling working life. And when it's your turn to be someone else's boss, you can make sure you don't inflict on others the miseries inflicted on you.

This book offers a lifeline for anyone suffering from a hostile work environment, and can help you transform the way you communicate and interact with others. It also contains a useful Personal Survival Kit, designed to help you really think about where you are and then take positive steps towards a happier, brighter, bastard-free future.

ISBN 978-1-904879-78-7
UK £9.99 / USA $17.95 / CAN $24.95

Leave The B@$T@*D$ Behind

An insider's guide to working for yourself

Richard Maun

☐ **Tick here if you've had enough**

CYAN

Marshall Cavendish
Business

Disclaimer

Please note: Any resemblance to any person or business contained within this book is purely coincidental. If you think you know someone in any of the examples, you are mistaken. I was writing about someone else, so hard luck.

Copyright © 2007 Richard Maun

First published in 2007 by:

Marshall Cavendish Limited
119 Wardour Street
London W1F 0UW
United Kingdom
T: +44 (0)20 7565 6000
F: +44 (0)20 7734 6221
E: sales@marshallcavendish.co.uk
Online bookstore: www.marshallcavendish.co.uk

and

Cyan Communications Limited
119 Wardour Street
London W1F 0UW
United Kingdom
T: +44 (0)20 7565 6120
E: sales@cyanbooks.com
www.cyanbooks.com

The right of Richard Maun to be identified as the author of this work has been asserted by him in accordance with the Copyright, Designs and Patents Act 1988.

A CIP record for this book is available from the British Library

ISBN-13 978-0-462-09899-9
ISBN-10 0-462-09899-0

Designed by Rick Sellars and typeset by Curran Publishing Services, Norwich, UK
Illustrations by Rebecca Maun, www.rmcs.co.uk

Printed and bound in Great Britain by
TJ International Ltd, Padstow, Cornwall

For Lucy and Theodore
You are loved, you have talent and you can choose your own path in life.

Contents

Preface

This is a book to help people make the transition from fed-up wage slave to enthusiastic self-employed free-man, or free-woman, whether your dream is to be a florist, a plumber, a consultant or any other gig where you don't report to an odious lump of a manager and where you are free from the shackles of an annual appraisal. A world where personnel managers are just a distant memory. A world where you can decide what sort of phone to buy and where you don't have to use it to report in to a lame duck bastard of a boss, because you don't have one of those any more.

These pages have not been lovingly crafted, printed and bound for people who want to borrow £5 million and buy an established business, or who already have wads of cash and just want to play at it. No, this book is aimed squarely at people like me who started with little more than an idea and a sense of self-belief that would have made the Angel Gabriel cough with surprise.

A clue to the content and style is in the title. Cunningly the book is not called *1001 Ways to Get Started* because you would fall asleep by the first chapter and probably consign the rest to the shredder. Instead it has the word 'bastard' in the title because when people make this kind of leap they are full of emotion and don't want to be force-fed lists of tip-top tips. What I wanted when I started was a book that would help me to understand some of the business basics, which make the difference between having fun and having a house. I wanted to read something that was informative and made me think, and that wasn't varnished by the dead hand of parental advice.

Most of the business books on my shelf are half-read because completing them is like trying to drive through a snowdrift without a steel snow plough bolted to the front of your car. No matter how hard you try, you just get bogged down and then have to wind down a window to let off a flare and be rescued. *Leave The Bastards Behind* comes without any snow-related safety kit, because it is breezy, pithy, informative and useful, so that you won't get stuck in the cold, wet, white stuff.

The world is full of bad language and it's fair to say that some of it has migrated into these pages, waiting quietly to be read, laughed at and thought about. If you're not the sort of person who likes to read a few naughty words then you have a choice. You can put the book back on the shelf or you can hand it to the person looking over your shoulder who doesn't have such hang-ups. I don't mind, because we all have choices to make in life and exercising your right to choose is what it's all about.

Choose to continue reading and you'll find some practical guidance to help you get going with your pet project. If you Google 'business books' you get a whopping 502,000,000 responses, but this is the only book to contain a handy height chart, some rude words about marketing types and a useful and unique personal planning kit. And if that wasn't enough, it even warns against the dangers of playing with fireworks.

Working for yourself is like sex. You can have fun, you can indulge your fantasies, but once you have fired the starting gun then there are going to be consequences, tears and a sticky patch. So this book is here to help. It's not intended to be a dull slog through the intricacies of discounted cash flow, the niceties of business law, or the pain of hiring help. Instead it covers the main issues people face when deciding to go it alone, and it invites them to think. I know, because I have worked for myself for over four years and so this book is part helpful companion and part reflections from the other side.

I have worked more hours than I ever worked when I was employed by someone else. I have had to learn fast to keep eating, and I have had days that have been so fantastically rewarding, I could have cried with the pleasure of just being me, doing what I wanted to do. On sunny days when I pull up to a client and park my car I still pinch myself that this is work. On the days when I'm stuck at home wading through accounts I also pinch myself that this is work, but the rough and the smooth is what makes life as a *selfer* so exhilarating and so stretching.

Read this book from cover to cover, and have fun working out for yourself *what* you will do and *how* you will start doing it for yourself. And if you are already in business, read it and think about all the decisions you can change now, and about all those little loose ends that you still haven't got to grips with. Then when you've finished it and completed the personal planning kit, if you want to spend some of your precious seed money on more books you have 502,000,000 choices to investigate. Life is always about choice, and *Leave The Bastards Behind* is here to help give you choices and invite you to consider your options. Have fun!

Whilst you're having fun, remember that no one is really a bastard. We might like to scapegoat our bosses for their bad behaviour, but as we own our own behaviour, we can choose to be powerful and do what we want to do. Think about the boss you hate. He (or she) may be overworked, under-trained and having to uphold a set of business objectives that he doesn't personally believe in, but being the boss he has to toe the party line or face the chop. Given the need to earn money to pay for life, it's inevitable that people's reaction to stress can be to treat their 'team' with harsh words and a short fuse. Don't pity them, simply think about how life must be for them, then focus on what you want to do for yourself and give them a cheery wave as you paddle off into the sunset.

There are no businesses that operate in a little bell jar, all on their own and isolated from the world around them, and it's the same with writing a book. Despite my sincere wish, this book did not arrive one morning in the post, completed, edited and ready to be read. So from my big jar of sweets I have some treats to hand out. First up is me, for actually managing to write the damn thing and for making sense of a pile of scribbles on odd bits of paper (loosely called planning). I'll have a rhubarb and custard sweet, I think.

Next up is my friend and chief supporter Harry Hemens, who has generously given me his experience when I needed it and who has listened patiently to my dribbling for many years. He gets a big round lollipop, as does Steve Tracey who lets me call him at odd times with crazy ideas, and who took the trouble of reading the drafts and giving me sincere and much-needed feedback. Thank you, chaps, and have a big lick on me. A chewy bar goes to Joe Holmes, who very kindly asked me a whole bunch of useful questions which got me thinking, and a big bag of jelly babies goes to the following supporters to share out and munch on: Julian Hammond, Alan Robertson, Frances Donnelly, Rob Godwin, David Jerram, Craig Walker, Mum and Bill, and the late and much missed John Morgan.

Finally a couple of bags of sherbet dip are reserved for Pom Somkabcharti and Martin Liu at Cyan. Without them, this would still be on my laptop, instead of in your hands. Enjoy all the sweets, everyone, and especially enjoy a tube of Daddy-Mints each, Lucy, Theodore and Rebecca, who have all helped me to become successful. If Newton stood majestically on the shoulders of giants, then I have perched on the wobbly shoulders of two small children and one hard-working wife. Thank you!

So if you fancy a dip into the world of 'after I had a proper job', complete with bad language and strong stories, then read on. Remember that you are responsible for all your choices, actions and inactions, because the responsibility to manage your own business sits squarely on your shoulders at all times. The book does reflect my genuine experience and is full of my failures and thoughts, but I don't intend to be sued, so keep your eyes open and your ears alert at all times. In addition, the examples have all been disguised, so that only I know who is really who, to save red faces and the threat of litigation.

Finally, if you're wondering why I bother to use strong words, then it's because life is like that – and don't pretend you didn't know them already!

Richard Maun

The Empty Desk
Leaving the bastards behind

1

I am fed up, frazzled and fucked off.

Not for the first time I find that my job has disappeared before my eyes. Evaporated in front of me like a will o' the wisp with a fast ticket out of here. This is not the first time this has happened, and I can feel a growing bubble inside me that says that this will be the last time. The last time I will have to sit opposite someone telling me he doesn't need me. The last time I will have to sit on my hands to avoid reaching out and squeezing his throat. The last time I will have to nod and smile and 'understand' that he just can't afford me any more.

Boss
It's nothing personal, you know, old chap. The chairman needs a new car and we wondered how the business was going to pay for it. And we thought ha! We could lose a Maun and *bingo*, we now have the money. So terribly sorry and all that, but you know, business is business. Would you like to see the brochure? It really is a very nice car, with leather seats and a special hook for curry bags. Car people are so clever these days. And the cup holders are the same ones that NASA uses on the shuttle.
Me
Don't they have a habit of blowing up?
Boss
Do they really? How fascinating. Anyway, Maun, there's an envelope for you. Only a small cheque. We're rather cash-strapped you see, just bought a new car. Oh, and there's the door. Do use it, please.
(*I tug a forelock and exit, stage left.*)
Boss
(*calls out*) Bye, Maun. Do have a nice life.
Me
(*I call back*) Thank you! (*Thinks: Fuck you!*)

Of course I haven't been told to my face that I'm being turned into a corporate love machine with burr walnut door handles and a cappuccino dispenser in the glove box, but the truth of it is that I might as well have been. Several years ago I found myself sitting in the meeting room at work, all alone and staring out into space, with tears in my eyes and that sinking feeling that life had just got a little bit more shit. And I pondered. And I felt the bubble, once dormant, now grow and surge and spring into life.

A smile spread across my face and I took a deep breath, wiped my eyes and decided that I was going to win this game. I was going to have a chair of my own which no one but me would sit in. A chair without surprises. A chair which would be loyal to me and which I would not find occupied by a fat, smiling executive, one cold morning without warning.

I was going into business. My business. It was time to build my boat, pack some provisions and set sail into the world of the self-employed. There was one question though, picking at the sleeve of my suit, like a small child in search of a sweet. Relentless and whining. The question was this:

Just what would my wife say when I told her of this bold decision?

Before we get to my wife and indeed many other helpful, loving and generally supportive people, let's stop and think about what this book is about. It's a book of personal stuff with useful bits, all about working for yourself. A personal story of what happened next, after I had made my decision. And unlike some of the less useful books on this subject, it will not stuff your head with a zillion ways to make a million, and it will not sit smugly in its corporate helicopter and tell you how to assemble a multi-level corporate strategy to take over the world. That kind of stuff may be useful, but I'm fed up with smug and patronising. This is the book I wish I'd had when I started. In the spirit of usefulness it will contain some thinking to encourage your thinking. It will contain some rude words, some interesting stories and some examples of how I fucked it up at times. See, a rude word already and we've only just begun.

I am successful, now.

I have survived. And I have enjoyed myself more in this gig than at any other time in my career so far, so we shall celebrate the good bits along the way. At the end of the book there is a very useful item for you to complete: your own personal planning kit. It's based in part on the business plan that I drew up for myself and used to guide me in the early days.

In my experience lots of small business types turn white when you ask them if they have a business plan. They all know that it makes sense to write things down, but there is a feeling that unless you have been to Harvard and can produce 40 pages of graphs and charts, then you are just playing at business. They are surprised when I show them my two-page plan, which I wrote in about half an hour. Often they say, 'Is that *it*?'

'What did you *expect*?' I reply. 'I haven't been to Harvard, don't have time to write 40 pages of business drivel, and am too lazy to plot any graphs. And I have carried this with me for 12 months and have ticked off all the elements.'

If you are already in business for yourself, use the personal planning kit to help you reflect on where you are now and where you want to walk to next week.

Life is full of shit sometimes, so we may as well have some fun on the way. Hence the bad language and the down-to-earth stories. Business can be like a small war, which is fought on the streets and in the hills. People get dirty and take bullet wounds. Sometimes they are fatal, sometimes they are not. People have to pull the trigger and get out there and mix it with the bad guys. Therefore, I am happy to share my mistakes, and if this helps one person to avoid taking a bullet in the heart, then the book will have done its job.

So having parked my wife we need to return to the action to find out what she said when I arrived home in a slightly mixed-up state. On the one hand I was relieved to be free from a company which had been sapping my energy and causing us all heartache. On the other hand I was now free of a salary, and I had a new house with a large mortgage, two small children and no obvious skills to sell.

However, I was also excited and had a gleam in my eye that I had not felt since the first term at university when everything was possible and life seemed so full of opportunities to have fun, get drunk and roll about with as many lady undergraduates as possible. After all nobody goes to Uni to learn. It's one of the great myths of our time. Like the fact that pensions will work out in the end (they won't) or the fact that plastic surgery can make you look like Britney (it won't).

My wife said nothing when I told her of my plan, decided upon just after lunch and padded out on the short drive home. She looked like she either wanted to cry with fear or hug me with hope. In fact she simply said:

'Oh.'

And then she said, 'What will we do for money?' And then we both burst into tears and hugged.

Big hairy life-changing events are chock-full of emotion, so we may as well face up to the fact that behind the thought that you will have your own business is a feeling. We do feelings in this book. And thinkings and doings. These are the three magic ingredients of life: think, feel and do. They work in the same way as a three-legged milking stool, and if you only ever balance on two legs you will, at some point when you least expect it, tip backwards into a pile of steaming cow plop and squirt milk up your nose.

Some people are not so good at feeling their feelings. They lock them away and present a granite exterior to the world. This can be very useful at times, particularly when you are selling to someone. Crying on the shoulder of a potential customer and dribbling tears down her jumper is a novel way of securing a deal, but it's not generally recommended. Developing a tough waterproof shell is a handy asset for being in business, but you need to take it off sometimes, let your soft inner underbelly flop out and own up to having some feelings.

It really is OK to let people know you are terrified and excited at the same time. That you are worried you do not have all the answers, or indeed all the questions. That you are embarrassed just by saying the words out loud: 'I want to work for myself, because I think I have some talent that people will buy into.' Some people are too modest for their own good. It's no fun having 'He died a modest man' engraved on your tombstone. That's too late to be of use. Instead it would be better to have, 'He died a happy man, who had a rich life and had a go at doing the things he really wanted to do.'

So *fuck* the modesty and think about what you really want to do. What is in your heart? What ambition lurks there that dare not speak its name? Like forbidden love and the need to get a thrill from the shopping channel.

Do remember that thinking is *work*. Your brain is a like a bulging bicep that goes flabby with under-use. Ask yourself this:

Is my brain the equivalent of a beer-swilling crisp-munching slob, or does it have the gleaming physique of a champion oarsman?

If your answer is nearer the slob end of things, then it's time to get into shape and have fun with mental squat thrusts. Give your frontal lobes a couple of laps round a cognitive cinder track, and a six-pack will soon be yours.

You can think. You might not do it very often, preferring constant action, like some sort of demented business paratrooper, who just can't help leaping out of the plane to sort things out. Relax and take off your jumpsuit and boots, because now is the time to read on, then go for a walk, make a fresh pot of tea and think about things.

It never ceases to amaze me that our culture is obsessed with doing. Doing stuff. Rushing to the shops to buy useless new gadgets and then rushing home again to watch sour-faced old biddies act in our favourite soap operas. We rush off to work and we rush off for a 'snatched' weekend break. If you're not doing something you must be dead or stupid. If we could all practise doing some quality thinking we might avoid some of the worst problems we encounter on a daily basis.

The same goes for business, where the general idea is often to check in your brain at the door and hang it on a peg next to your coat. You won't be needing it for the next eight hours, so best to leave it in a safe place. Most of the guilt for this attitude is shouldered by the senior management, who despite having a clutch of degrees, MBAs, and having been through leadership training that would make an eight-year-old yawn, decide en masse to deploy a new corporate policy which has all the merits and profit potential of a dead llama. The cult of the consensus board, or the decisions rubber-stamped by a tame management committee, who are too weak or cowardly to stand up to the wretched tyrant at the top, is a disgrace.

Think of the famous corporate names who have sold sure-fire winning businesses in order to invest in technology, or who have paid five times the market price for a licence to peddle as yet unknown items. Think of the sports teams that are financed by big shots with more in their trousers than their brains, who spend vast fortunes to build the killer pub quiz team, only to find out that a 20,000 seat capacity pub is a tricky thing to fill.

If only some of these people had some of the time stopped to think, then perhaps some of the world and most of the pension funds wouldn't be headed for meltdown.

There are exceptions to this: those talented few who don't talk through their backsides. Who ponder and stop and smell the daisies and carefully work out their next move. These organizations are the modern equivalents of the Great Pyramids. Their organizations are massive, stable, profitable and designed to be around for at least a thousand years. Perhaps even one day there will be a token two or three mega global businesses that have sucked up all the others in the way that gravity from a black hole sucks up light.

So when I made that tiny little decision to do something different, I was thinking for *myself*. I was thinking about what I would really, *really* like to do.

Because people have a nasty habit of forgetting things in the heat of the moment, the personal planning kit at the back of the book can be cut out and tucked under your wing for when that crucial moment arrives. And you will know when that is, because a tiny little thought will sidle up to the first domino in the long, long line of dominoes stretching round your brain and give it a sharp kick in the ribs. Clack-clack-clack, down they fall and whoopee – off we go, heading towards the land of the *selfer*.

However, let's remember that my story is mine. Yours will be yours. Therefore you are cheerfully invited to say *bollocks* to any part you disagree with, and to choose a way for yourself that works. My way worked for me; you are *you* and need to be responsible for your way. Because you are responsible to yourself and that is the way life is.

Stop at this point and think about what it is you would like to do:

- Set up as a hairdresser?
- Move to becoming a contract electrician?
- Chuck in the corporate towel and become a consultant?
- Go freelance?
- Buy a franchise?
- Set up as a therapist?
- Make money as a masseuse?
- Open a shop?
- Retrain as a ... (you decide)?
- Or a thousand other opportunities to stop working for other people and discover the satisfaction doing it for yourself.

It's OK to dream and to be talented at something. It's OK just to want to have a go at avoiding spending the rest of your life as a barfly who moans that he could have been *the* man, if only he had listened to his heart. I met a pensioner once at a rugby club bar in Wales. He had sat quietly in a corner while I moaned to a friend that I couldn't do what I wanted. The old gent then leaned over and said, 'Look, sonny, I'm 78 and you don't want to be sitting here like me, wishing you had done things. Think about it.' His eyes sparkled and he held his gaze steady, which although was slightly unnerving also made me concentrate. After thanking him politely, I found on the walk home that I really was chewing on his comments, and that he had scored a direct hit on the bit of me that wants to lead a life and not just be a follower.

There is a small part of our hearts which is like a tiny happy flea sitting on a deckchair, quietly reading a newspaper under the warming sun. This little flea is our life force, that bit of us that gets up sometimes and says, 'Hang on, I want to do this for me.' Or 'I have a dream' or 'Will you stop doing that?' or 'I will lead my life for me.' Most of the time the flea is just happy to sit and read and perhaps doodle a bit on the crossword puzzle.

Sometimes however, a breeze makes him look up and stirs him into life. He throws down his paper and springs and twists around in the air, doing what he wants to do, just for himself. And so it was that the old man's comments were like a breeze which stirred up my own flea. Then many years later when I was older and wiser (or more stupid, depending on your viewpoint) and my job had been taken away from me, the shock and shame and hurt of it also stirred up the flea, who rolled up his newspaper and jumped and jumped and jumped and made big divots in the sand, which read, 'Follow your heart.'

So I did.

With only a biro and my ex-company car for company, I struck out on my own as a business coach. Quickly building on my existing industrial experience, I added new skills at my own expense, and in the early days, when I was still greener than a slice of tropical rain forest, cut the odd corner to stay one step ahead of the clients. Working for myself really rammed home the sentiment, borrowed from the lawless gun-toting Wild West, that:

In business there are the quick and there are the dead.

I determined to be quick.

Sitting in the smoky depths of a franchised pub and 'restaurant', I almost never made it past my first day on the job. Nervous, unsure of myself, but ballsy enough to be there anyway, my first client sat in front of me, his eyes unblinking with suspicion and his bulging arms folded stoutly. He looked at me as if I was a bug sitting on the rim of his beer glass, and grunted belligerently, 'Wot ya goona do for me then?'

I smiled and said coaching wasn't like that, and that it was about working together. While I fumbled to convince both of us that I knew what the hell I was talking about, he abruptly stood up and nipped to the toilets. Seizing my chance, I reached into my jacket pocket, pulled out a small book on coaching and speed read as much as I could in the three minutes he was gone. Hearing the toilet door bang open, I stopped and just managed to squeeze it back into my pocket as he sat down again. I smiled at him, with a secret smugness because my quick mental freshen-up had done the trick. I now had some words in my head and a fresh clip of questions to fire at him.

During that first session we talked through several improvement options, and he quickly worked out how he could save £50,000 in his business. The client and the conversation both relaxed, and I was off and away. Thanks in part to his need to empty his bladder, and in part to a small book tucked in my pocket.

A friend of mine said that 'You can fake it until you can make it.' And I have been guilty of sailing close to the wind several times in the early days. Sometimes when under pressure I would suggest to the client that it was her turn to buy the coffee, and while she was at the counter I would do a hurried spot of revision. A bit cheeky perhaps, but when you're on your own you need to be resourceful.

It's a Catch-22 really, because you need experience and you can only get *that* by having a go. Sometimes you just have to hold your breath and dive into the water.

When I started to facilitate training workshops for clients, I was still being trained myself, and I would book the workshop for the week after my own training. This would give me a couple of days to prepare, and as the training was fresh in my head I would sail through and appear knowledgeable and confident. The reality was that I spent the first six months wetting myself that I would be found out and exposed as a 'fraud'. Not that I was doing anything fraudulent, just that people hate being told, 'Thanks for being my first client, and I wish us *both* good luck today.'

A chum reminded me that when you are training people, you are OK as long as you stay one page ahead of the delegates. On one memorable occasion I was down to my last half-page of advance notes before we stopped for a break and I could swot up on the next section.

Today, I am an experienced and confident coach and trainer, but without taking a few risks in business I would never have made it. You too can cut a few corners if you need to, as long as you're not doing anything illegal or unsafe. Of course, if you are a freelance brain surgeon I would tend to suggest you don't apply this helpful rule of thumb and make sure you get properly qualified before slicing open your first head.

Before we pause and turn to the personal planning kit, let's take a moment to think about what sort of business you would like. I started as a *sole trader*, where you and the business are one and the same. The business's money is your money, and the risk is your risk. Sole trading is quick and simple to set up, and I was advised to voluntarily register for VAT in order to look more professional. Remember, kids, that VAT paid to you is not yours, and that when you register you become an unpaid tax-collection service. On the upside, you can reclaim VAT spent on your start-up costs, and so it is well worth considering.

After a couple of years I incorporated my business into a *limited company* and put 'Ltd' after my name. Limited companies are more expensive to set up, and more complex to run, than sole-trading businesses, because the company is a separate legal entity. Getting your money out is harder, but can be more tax-efficient and this is one of the attractions of going limited.

Lastly there are *partnerships*, which are a bit like a limited company with a pre-nuptial agreement. Partnerships are also a legal entity, and if you're thinking of forming one it's essential to draw up a partnership agreement, or you could be dropped in a dung heap should you need to dissolve the arrangement in the future.

Whichever option you choose, sole trader, limited company or partnership, it pays to get some tax advice and to think about the costs involved in setting them up and winding them down.

Pause here for a moment. Think about what you would like to do, and don't let a lack of skills or experience get in your way. Then turn to the back of the book where the Personal Planning Kit is sitting waiting for you. Please complete the first section called 'A Sense of the Future' (on page 160). As you don't have to show it to anyone for now, just go for broke. What's in your heart? Don't worry about fear or practicality; if you edit your dreams then your life is going to be a bit short on fulfilment. Laugh, smile to yourself and go for it. Then when you're happy with your answers come back here and continue.

Now you have put some words to your dreams it's time to dive into the word of the selfer and have fun, so without pausing for refreshment let's leave our corner-cutting behind us and think about keeping our bottom in good shape.

And I don't mean through liposuction.

A Happy Bottom
How to avoid a business spanking

2

Let's give some shape to the book. On the journey from miserable fed-up wretch behind an empty desk to a happy, worried, excited puppy behind a differently empty desk you need to consider some overall themes. Although these are embedded in each chapter it is worth collecting them up in one place so that you can see them and tuck them into your conscious memory. Keeping things in sight is a good idea, and the fun way to do this is to drum up an acronym. You know: the sort of thing that experts at conferences always intimidate you with, having spent 10 years researching at the School of Flaky Management, department of Advanced Acronyms.

Some of these people are gurus and spend their sad lives living at the top of a saintly management pole. Some of them live in the real world and enrich our working lives with their shrewd observations. However, increasingly there is a tendency for people to forget that there is as much bollocks and showmanship in management and business theory as there ever was in a nineteenth-century travelling vaudeville show. Gasp at the latest theory, applaud the business boffin with a bad perm, or jot down the latest buzz word in your executive PDA. PT Barnum would be proud.

Because a selfer needs to work to eat, we need to keep things simple. If your business is loaded onto a PDA and it breaks, you're shagged. If you drop your diary it will bounce. If you drop your PDA it will break. Your business will break with it, and don't kid yourself that you will have backed everything up, because in my experience people can be really slack about this.

Business is not and does not have to be complicated. If the pyramids were built without batteries and the Wright Brothers pioneered powered flight without the use of SatNav and an arm-rest television, your business can be built from the ground up in the most simple, cost-effective way possible. Keep business simple. Even airline pilots are selected on the basis of having one big thumb, which they use to switch on the autopilot. If you make life all complicated and squiggly on day one, you will load down your poor old biplane with a drinks trolley, and mess it up. And if you do that, you will get spanked. But not in a sexy way. No sir, you'll get spanked in a way that will leave your bottom sore for six months.

Before you go onto the internet to look up spank, spanking or spanked – and I suggest you don't if there are kiddies in the room – (so I'm told) what we have here is a word designed to knit together the key themes that you have to be mindful of in order to power your business off the foggy runway of hope and into the inky blue sky of your dreams. The word has been carefully machined out of an ingot of pure usefulness. It's a word you will remember, an acronym to fling at people with cheery abandon, in order to combat some of the more sterile and no less contrived acronyms currently polluting the world of business.

Our word is SPANK and the bottom-smackingly relevant themes are:

S **Self** – you are the talent and the key limiting factor on your business.
P **Planning** – plan for cash, for uncertainty, for busy periods and for rainy days.
A **Assumptions** – you will live or die by the ones you make.
N **Networking** – get on your bike and tell the world you exist.
K **Kick ass** – whip up your motivation, drive and determination and then let rip.

Self comes first because you are your business, and its level of success or failure is directly attributable to what you think, feel and do.

If you **plan**, then the risk of sudden cash shortages is reduced, time is made better use of, and people tend not to find themselves buying the Christmas turkey at Easter.

I shall make an **assumption** here: that we all make assumptions: such as that people who say they are successful must be telling the truth, that people who are told a price assume it is the lowest price on offer, and that to be successful you need at least four business degrees in assorted flavours. All of these assumptions are, to borrow a phrase, horseshit.

After assumptions we have **networking**, the big shh ... you know what, which we shall return to in a later chapter.

Finally we have **kick ass** because to work for yourself, in whatever capacity, means taking pot-shots at the market place so that you stamp out your presence and start to win customers.

To return to assumptions, it is easy to say 'check out your assumptions' and tougher to do it. They are sneaky snakes which slide up our trousers without us noticing, until their little fangs bite into our soft parts, with devastating results. You could wear bicycle clips at all times to keep the reptiles out, but they might just draw some curious looks from those not in the know. To avoid sartorial embarrassment, think about the following general assumptions which I have heard from several clients. Which ones do you recognize?

If I set up in business people will buy my products or services.
Answer: why the hell should they, when there are perfectly reasonable people already providing the same thing already?

When I am in business it's OK to put all my receipts in a shoe box and leave them there until year end.

Whoa there, horsey. I don't know any accountants who use shoe boxes, so take a tip from them. The accounting shoe box is the business equivalent of a Christmas present from Great Aunt Monolith: you know, the one with the goatee and the pulsating wart. At some point you are going to have to open both the box and the present, and who knows what disasters will be waiting for you. At least with the Great Aunt all you have to do is kiss her. This is much more pleasant than shovelling through a pile of receipts at year end, because your Great Aunt is not going to bankrupt you, whereas ignorance of your cashflow could.

Be warned. Ignorance makes a poor business partner, and without cash you will have to give old Monolith a big tonguey one to keep your baby business afloat. Yuk! We shall return to the perils of the shoe box at the end of the book, with a couple of cautionary tales to do with business accounting.

People will buy my products for the price I ask.

Be careful. If you want to sell a bunch of flowers for £10 and everyone else sells them for £8, then either you will sell nothing, or you will have to think of a way to justify your price. When you work out how much you need to sell your products for, it pays to salt your numbers with some local research, or to reduce your optimism to avoid a nasty surprise.

I know how much it will cost to set up and run my business.

No you don't. You can have a guess and add 20 per cent to be cautious, because things in life always seem to cost more. Every time I go to the supermarket, intent on picking up a few essentials, I always come away with more than I need, but just the right amount that I want. I'm a sucker for 'new' things and for shiny packaging. Have you noticed how the price of items is not on the packet itself? Once the goods are in your trolley you have no idea how much the bill is going to be, and business can be the same. Despite your best intentions to be frugal there is always something extra to buy. I have spent about 10 times more on personal training than I ever thought I would need to. It's money well spent, just not money well budgeted for!

Be cautious and always add in some sort of contingency. I mean, you would if you were having the builders round, wouldn't you?

My family has the stamina to go through with it.
Hmm ... Don't overlook the fact that the people closest to you will invest emotionally in your business. Don't assume that you have enough credit in the Bank of Family to allow you to fund your venture. Talk to them and find out how much time they will support you for, or whether they are prepared to see little of you whilst you toil away to get things going. Or how happy they are that you're going to delay buying the latest high-definition, fold-away flat-screen television and combined drinks cabinet because you need to spend the money on a big roll of packing tape.

From the moment you push the go button on your new venture, you keep drawing on your credit at the Bank of Family, and if this gets overstretched they may just call in the debt. If they do that, the emotional bailiffs will come round and will repossess your heart.

To be successful in business we all need to have happy bottoms, and that means not getting spanked. When I started out I made most of the above assumptions, didn't think about my own limitations enough, planned only for the next six months, nearly drowned in assumptions, avoided networking and only kicked ass when my wife kicked ass with me. And I made some assumptions – did I mention that?

My original business plan had me working only as a coach. To be successful I needed 20 clients a month who would all pay me the same amount. I didn't think about the cost of running my car, the difficulty of finding and maintaining such a client list, and even the time taken to research, interview and win new customers. I assumed that it would all fall into place. I even nearly turned down a chance to join a networking group, on the grounds that I was a) scared to talk to people and b) found the idea somehow beneath me. Then just to rub salt into a raw wound, I proudly announced to my wife that I would do nothing for three months, whilst I qualified in psychometric profiling.

I had no idea how much in love I was with my big plan, and completely missed the reality of it all. However, once the money started to flow out of the house and the bills began to stack up, I realized a fundamental truth about business: you can't sell if you are sitting at home in front of your laptop. So I went out selling and never looked back.

All of this was extracting credit from my Bank of Family at a hideous rate, and although I'm successful today, I'm still paying off the emotional overdraft that I racked up to keep the bailiffs away. It hurts!

Stop here and catch your breath.

There are two things to add to your personal planning kit. They are to do with the assumptions you are making and the amount of credit you have with those closest to you.

It might help to grab a biscuit and a hot milky drink here to sustain you through your thinking. You might also want to fiddle with some rough numbers and see whether they add up and your business looks viable, or in business argot, whether it has legs. The profit you will make is the total income you generate from sales less the cost of running your business. Remember that until you've been in business a year, you don't really know these numbers.

Please don't fall into the trap of working out all your costs first and then just add on enough sales to cover them, because people who do this tend to have a nasty habit of buying luxury cars, oak-veneered shop interiors, Gucci toolboxes, or thermo-nuclear powered laptops.

Given that lots of business people have failed at some point, but only talk about their successes, it is likely that you will only ever hear good news from them. I have seen some people go bankrupt, and others come close, because they made silly mistakes and fell in love with their dream, instead of falling in love with the harsh reality of being a *selfer*. As the sages have it:

Business is business. If you want a friend, get a dog.

I like this and would add:

Don't get spanked. Get wise and keep your bottom happy.

Pause here and ponder on the need to avoid a *spanking*. Then turn to section 2 in your Personal Planning Kit, called 'Assumptions and Bank of Family' (on page 162). Write down the assumptions you are making and find out how much emotional credit you have to draw on.

So there I was, at home again with no job and possible success just a whistling train in the distance. A train that might or might not come puffing into my station on time. Bugger!

Except this time I was excited and full of hope. The world had stopped turning for a moment and all around was silence. I had decided to stop working for other people and instead to embark on a journey which would swing between the highest of highs and the lowest of lows, sometimes all on the same day and occasionally in the same hour.

Then the spell was broken by my wife, who looked around the smart new house that we had moved into only six months before, and said sadly, 'I suppose this will have to go.'

You You You
What sort of firework are you?

Benjamin Disraeli has been quoted as saying that there are three kinds of lies: lies, damned lies and statistics. This could be the most profound thing that anyone has said in the history of business. Sadly however, he never actually muttered those particular words. Mark Twain only said that he did, and in all probability the quote can be attributed to Leonard H. Courtney, who was overheard mumbling it in 1895. As any schoolboy knows, Lenny, as he was popularly known, went on to become the President of the Royal Statistical Society. It's a society whose members aren't noted for their ability to get smashed and play table rugby, but they do still insist on calculating the winner of the Christmas raffle to six decimal places.

Given that lots of business failures are attributable to the use and abuse of numbers so dodgy that if they turned up to take your daughter out for a date, you would grab your shotgun and shout, 'Now git offa ma land' at them, it pays to look at all business numbers through extremely dark glasses, to avoid being blinded by their cheeky smug grins.

However, one statistic which is probably true is that one in two businesses fail in their first two years.[1] A whopping 50 per cent bite the dust, and take a large slice of investment capital with them.

A statistic that I made up, purely to stimulate thinking, is that 99.6 per cent of all these business failures are attributable to the person who set up the business in the first place. The other 0.4 per cent are down to alien invasion, meteorite impact, or a sudden and unexpected win at the international super-lottery, followed by a lifetime of persecution by money-grabbing charities and bleeding heart cases.

---

1   Source: The Times online, www.thetimes100.co.uk

The point is this. If you are in business it is your business. It is chock full of your strengths and talents – and weaknesses and blind spots. Stir in some prejudices and useless received wisdom, and you can quickly draw the boundaries to your entrepreneurial world.

For example, I knew a salesman who insisted that he did not call on new prospects on a Friday, because that was not the done thing. I pointed out to him that I was a prospect, and that actually Friday was a very good day to call, as my week was behind me and I had often had time to listen to a new pitch. He was adamant that this was not what *professional* sales people did. Perhaps there is a sales law that says, 'Thou shalt rest on the fifth day.' I don't buy this myself. If this person had been working for himself, he would have lost 20 per cent of his selling time, simply because he believed something which was not true. Given the increasing competition businesses face on all fronts, it seems ludicrous to cut yourself short, but that's just what people do.

If I had my time over again, I would not spend three months scaring my wife witless by sitting at home 'preparing'. I would get a second job to make ends meet, and I would spend time visiting people. The result of my apparent laziness, largely through being nervous about meeting new people, is that I drew heavily on my credit at home and spent more of my meagre savings than I really needed to.

It wasn't a great start, but now I enjoy my work, like meeting people, and have sold and sold and sold. However, I used to be a shit salesman. Terrified that I would disappear in the darker parts of a major city and never be found again, except for a hubcap and a couple of ribs, I stayed home and kept myself safe.

The best way to learn fast is not to have a salary and still have some kids and a goldfish to feed. Ask yourself the following questions:

- What skills do I need to polish in order to survive?
- How long have I got before Bubbles (the goldfish) starves?

Selling skills, or lack of them, is the reason that 51 per cent of all people who would go into business don't do so. Another 32 per cent don't do it because they are just generally scared, and the remaining 17 per cent claim they cannot raise the finance. Play with the numbers if you like, as I made them up myself to stimulate discussion. There are loads of reasons not to do something. When you stop and think about it, most people are *already* in business for themselves.

They're in the family business.

They run a house worth thousands, nurture small children, buy and sell at markets and car boot fairs, organize stock in the fridge, cope with arduous family Christmases and navigate themselves around the world on sun-drenched holidays. If you're pondering on whether you dare you go into business, ponder no longer. Look around you at your home life: you're already there!

Motivation is essential. If you have it, you will do well. If you don't, then you're toast. Badly burnt toast at that.

A brown bear can hibernate for months through the winter because he has a tummy full of picnics and packed lunches. He has the energy on board to sustain him through lean times. Think of yourself as a brown bear. Do you have sufficient fat reserves to keep you going through the hard slog of starting your business? If you needed an interview to get the job of florist, gardener, electrician or freelance musician, would you have enough passion and motivation to convince someone else to hire you?

I've had a fair few job interviews and mostly found them boring, because the jobs were boring. My best ever interview answer was, to a lifeless grey human resources manager, 'That's a nice car.' (I was gazing out of the window). He replied, 'Thank you, it's mine.' So I asked him why he chose it. I couldn't be bothered to ask a decent question, because my motivation had all leaked away down the sleeve of my suit while he droned on about procedures and targets and that if I was a good boy I might get promoted in 10 years time.

When I started working for myself I first had to pass a tough interview – with myself. The interview went something like this:

Maun
So, Richard, I see that you've applied to work for yourself. As your subconscious I've had a look at our CV and can see there's potential. So what brings you here, my boy?
Me
Yes – er, hello, subconscious. I have decided to change direction. You know, set up my own business and be my own boss.
Maun
(*looking suspicious*) Hmm … Why did you apply?
Me
Because I am fed up with losing my job, with having crappy appraisals, with being told what to do by people who take no responsibility for their own shortcomings, with having to live with shit decisions made by others, and with having to get up, shave, shower, suit up, drive 40 miles to sit behind a desk and spend the day typing a deathly dull report, when I could have done all that at

home in my shorts, feeling relaxed and skipping the banal banter of office life.

Maun

I see. These are all rather negative points. Are there any positives?

Me

Of course. I want to choose for myself when I have lunch. I want to go shopping after I have met with a client (instead of reporting in like an errant schoolboy). I want to learn new things that I am interested in. I want to work hard doing something that really satisfies me. I want to have my own chair which is never going to be occupied by someone who has just elbowed me out of it, and finally, as I am going to be in work for the next 30 years, I WANT TO ENJOY THE BLOODY THING!

Maun

So you have thought about it. I like what you have to say and am thinking of inviting you back for a second interview.

Me

(*confused*) What? Two interviews? For my own job? With myself!

Maun

Well, as your subconscious, I have to be sure. I don't want to make a mistake. There might even be a psychometric profile. Your yin and yang are arguing about the need as we speak. Do you have any questions?

Me

Psychometrics – you rotten swine! I thought you were supposed to me on my side!

Maun

What? Of course I'm on *our* side, if you're up to the job. And let me say, we are very impressed by your passion and energy. It's a good sign. The best, even.

Me
Oh well, fair enough. And you said 'we' – is there more than one of me?

Maun
There could be. We are complex beings, you know. Perhaps a decent salesperson lurks beneath your lazy exterior.

Me
Thanks very much. Even my subconscious is having a go at me!

Maun
Don't take it personally. I'm just being honest with you, my boy. Anyway, as I said, we do like your passion.

Me
That's good. So I've got the job?

Maun
No, not yet. However, I have now decided to invite you back for a second interview, after you've thought a bit more about yourself.

Me
Thank you, you're too kind.

Maun
And you can cut the sarcasm: this is still a job interview. Now, let me explain about the dangers of playing with fireworks.

The Fireworks Code

The Chinese have been credited with inventing many things, including the seismograph, money, kites and Indian ink. Given that these on their own would have }led to a pretty dull social scene, they also livened things up by inventing spaghetti, whisky and brandy, and then realizing that they had a bunch of drunk, but well fed, partygoers to trundle home, they invented the wheelbarrow. After that they never looked back, although had they looked to the left on the map they would have realized their parties were going to be the best in the world for nearly two thousand years.

They also invented gunpowder and fireworks, and eventually the Fireworks Code, which basically says that you'd be foolish to let a bunch of drunken Chinese mess about with fireworks when raising hell with their wheelbarrows.

Every year we love to play with this entertaining kind of high explosive, either during annual celebrations of long-dead traitors, or at someone's special anniversary party, or at dull weddings. As kids we are told firmly that children should not play with fireworks, and that only a responsible adult should handle them. The 'responsible adult' in question is invariably a dad, who sticks them in old beer bottles, tries to light three at a time with the stub of a cigarette, or who takes great pride in aiming his giant space-death rockets at the neighbour's greenhouse, in a scene based largely on his schoolboy learning about the Battle of Waterloo. Clearly dads are more of a liability than well-mannered children, and the mums cluck and tell their offspring to ignore their lunatic fathers, who are all single-handedly trying to defeat the imaginary French in one massive drunken barrage.

Setting up in business is a lot like playing with fireworks. They might go whoosh and explode in a show of rainbow sparks, but they might also explode in your face or just be rather a dull waste of money. Imagine that you are a firework, tucked into the box of Dad's Special Howitzer Attack Selection. You have kinetic energy stored up, and once the blue paper has been touched you will pop and fizz and bathe in the 'Oohs' and 'Aahs' of the people who love you the most.

Knowing what sort of firework you are is helpful because it keeps you aware of your personal style when under pressure. This is useful because people can waste effort in the early days, not because they are stupid, but because they tend to go back to old patterns of behaviour when under stress. Going into business can be one of the most stressful things to do in life, after paying the gas bill, cooking Christmas dinner for an assortment of hyper-critical old relatives, or trying to squeeze your stomach into a dangerously tight swimsuit when next on the beach.

Identifying your own particular type of behaviour is easy. Simply ask your wife, partner or casual weekend lover (or all three if you're that lucky) to answer the following questions:

> **Question 1.** When under pressure do you tend to think deeply about the problem, or do you just switch off your brain to prevent overheating and let someone else do the thinking for you?
> **Question 2.** When under pressure do you rush about using up energy, or do you lapse into a worried trance?

Question 1 is about thinking style, and how much you use your brain. Question 2 is about movement, and whether you tend to have any. However, when under stress we can go into extreme behaviours, and therefore our energy or thinking can be over-used or misplaced, which can waste time or money or both. If you're stuck about where you are, then consider these two scales:

A Thinking

Quick, or shallow thinking	– 1 2 3 4 5 6 7 8 9 10 –	Deep thinking, or fixated thinking

B Activity

Inactivity, or sluggish movement	– 1 2 3 4 5 6 7 8 9 10 –	Train-track direction, or shotgun approach

Put a ring round the number that best describes you on each scale, when you're under severe pressure. Note there is no middle point, to avoid you going for an easy half-way mark. People tend lean towards either end, when under pressure. Then look at the Firework Model of Stress and think about which section you sit in, which will be down to a combination of the answers to the two questions and your marks on the scales.

Firework Model of Stress (FMoS)

BEHAVIOUR	Lazy Activity	Hyper Activity
Hyper Thinking	Catherine Wheel — Round in circles	Rocket — Lost in space
Lazy Thinking	Damp squib — Fizzle out...	Fountain — Shotgun Approach

The four fireworks represent the four types of behaviour that others will see us doing at the start of our self-employed life, and also more generally when faced with a stressful situation. None of them are terribly useful to us, and that is often the way, when we get overloaded with the enormity of the situation.

The temptation here is to chuckle and notice that *none* of the four styles are *exactly* like you. If you do, then watch out: you could be in for a big fall at some point. It's much better to laugh out loud and find yourself in the model. We don't care toffee about exactitude here: just realize that you are not some kind of perfect super-being and acknowledge which firework best describes you. Think of this kind of knowledge as an insurance policy against future fuck-ups. Know yourself and be open to a bit of self-learning. It can only ever help.

Often, after a messy encounter with Doctor Stress we find ourselves saying, 'Oh why did I do that again?' which is a sure sign that we have just defaulted to some old behaviour which we have developed to keep ourselves safe, but which now gets in our way. These kinds of behaviour tend to develop in the early years of childhood, when the task in hand was tidying our bedroom, or learning to paint with our fingers. Our style didn't seem to matter then, it just kept us 'safe' from being told off by parents, teachers or nosy neighbours.

We soon learned what to do, or not do, in order to keep the peace. We also learned techniques for those times when we felt like making damn sure we secured the undivided attention of our elders. Some kids play dumb, others argue back, a few scream and howl tears of rage. Some do lots of things in the hope that one of them is right; some do nothing to avoid getting anything wrong. This is all part of the richly textured life we lead, and does not make us 'mad, bad and dangerous to know'.

Unlike George Gordon Byron – better known as Lord B – who was described as all of these things by his ex-lover Lady Caroline Lamb,[2] around the early 1800s. In terms of decadent one-upmanship Byron was in a class of his own. He claimed to have slept with over 250 women in Venice, in just one year. Had he lived today he would have been the sole source for several disgustingly frank kiss-and-tell magazines, and would have hosted his own TV game show, called most probably, 'If it moves, bonk it.'

We are who we are, and we cannot turn back the clock, as several hundred of Byron's ex-lovers probably wished they could have done. We are good, special people, full of positive intentions, and we all have a right to a happy life, a right to learn about ourselves and a right to make new decisions about how to act or react.

Therefore, knowing which type of firework best describes you is not something to feel guilty or embarrassed about. No way! Feel proud that you have identified yourself, and are now in a much stronger position to make progress than the person down the road, who might just fail through ignorance of his or her own shortcomings.

The four different firework types all represent a particular way of reacting to stress. Too much, or too little, thinking or activity can cause problems for people, especially if they go unchecked.

First up we have the **damp squib**. For these people the word 'half' features a lot in their lives – half-hearted or half-baked, for example. Damp squibs go into business on the back of someone else's prodding, and they lack the

---

2 Source: 'George Byron, 6th Baron Byron', Wikipedia. It's a free resource so why not use it?

determination to move beyond the initial rush of excitement. They tend to waste money on investigating new projects, perhaps even buying some kit or dabbling with a bit of training, and they may have a long history of so nearly achieving something. The worst thing a damp squib can do is actually to go into business. Their lack of thinking, combined with their lack of activity, is a sure sign of a disaster waiting to happen. You know when you've met a damp squib because they complain about their current project and say things like 'It's so hard to get going. Nobody wants me.' This is code for 'I haven't really tried and my quick thinking wasn't developed enough to come up with anything of substance.' On Fireworks Night the damp squib in the box promises so much, but delivers nothing other than a flat fart of tired resignation.

Damp squibs by their nature tend not to appear very often in the circle of local businesses, and if they do, then you only see them once, before their energy dissipates and they go and find a 'proper job'. A number of colleagues I know make regular noises about working for themselves, but fortunately don't take the leap. If this could be you too, then don't act on someone else's nagging. Only set up your business when your inner drive burns a hole through your carpet slippers. Otherwise you're heading for a miserable time. Don't fret about it though; life has other things in store for you.

Fountains on the other hand are much more magnificent. They spew sparks in all directions and make a right mess of your lawn. In business terms a fountain is someone who tends to prefer action to thinking. In fact there's a reasonable chance fountains will invite someone else to do their thinking for them.

They also have a nasty habit of latching on to the latest new idea. Fountains have three new ideas before breakfast and start working on them all before lunch, before getting bored and wandering off to test some more things before tea. They leave a debris trail of half-finished starts, and can waste money on a prodigious scale, in their attempt to find the magic thing that will really work for them. Sadly though, their lack of thinking means that each bright new dawn is shortly followed by the sudden arrival of intellectual dusk, and they soon lose interest.

Fountains can be heard saying things like 'I know I said I would do that, but I've just had a much better idea.' A fountain will try anything once, as it could be good for business. The result of this is that they tend to diversify too quickly and can offer a muddled selection of products or services. They might be successful if one of their ideas manages to take root in the market place, but the pressure of constantly firing out in new directions can take a toll on their overall success.

I knew a fountain who set up a business to sell car alarms, and then invested in electronic garage doors. The last time I met her she was setting up an internet business to sell time shares in some far-flung holiday wasteland. Each idea was going to be the big one, and each new phase passed swiftly and drained away another chunk of her financial resources.

If you sound like a fountain, then the key is to budget carefully and honestly, so that you're not tempted to spend money or time following up dead-end ideas. Invite someone you trust to be a partner or a mentor, and act on his or her feedback. If you don't, then you could end up with a business which has many body parts to it, but not enough to make a whole person.

Catherine wheels are undoubtedly fascinating, as they spin faster and faster and then burn themselves out, leaving a plate-sized scorch mark on your lapped pine fence. They like to think deeply about everything, which to them is as natural and obvious as breathing. To the outside world it looks like madness. Their hyper-thinking style means that they over-think. They mine a deep shaft of ideas and possibilities for each new element in their business, and just when you think they've thought enough, they do a little bit more. They can polish a good idea so hard that it soon becomes worn down to a stub and is spoiled. Before they actually do anything they tend to say, 'Um – hang on a minute. I'll need to think about that first.'

Hyper thinking for them is the equivalent of a rushing river scouring out a deep canyon. It's impressive, but dangerous. Having thought about it (notice the clue), I have to hold my hand up to being a catherine wheel. Concerned that I might make a mistake and be thought less of by people, I spent hours designing my business card and my marketing leaflets, making sure that each dot was in the right place and that each word had passed its rigorous entry exam. I laugh about it now, but at the time it was no joke. When we talk about marketing later on, I shall reveal just how many times I tweaked my business card. It's more than five.

Catherine wheels love to explore all the possibilities in their head, which means considering both the upside and the downside of lifting a finger, or scratching their backside. Invited to a join a networking group I mulled it over for far too long, and only signed up when I was asked how I would feel if someone else took my place. Concerned that a competitor would steal my chair and my business, I promptly wrote a cheque for the joining fee and delivered it right away.

If you fit into the catherine wheel square on the model, then you run the risk of spending six months refining your business plan before getting out of your chair and meeting people. The antidote is to give yourself a limit to your thinking time and to stick with it. It's OK to be good enough; it really is. A client spotted a tiny typo in one of my leaflets once, and still booked me! Can you believe it!? I was so surprised I nearly fell off my chair (while quietly wringing my hands at my error). Perfection doesn't exist, and trying to reach for it only spoils the good things you already have in front of you.

Finally we have the **rocket**, the sort of person who has hyper-thinking and hyper-activity. Unlike the catherine wheel, who could think you to death at 20 paces, rockets latch on to one idea and then focus exclusively on it, ignoring any evidence that could help them come to a balanced judgement. They only see positive things, unlike the catherine wheel who is great at seeing negative stuff. Rockets feel like they have been given a one-way ticket to success, and there's a strong pull to start right now.

Rockets tend to zoom off in one direction and keep going until way past the point where they should have stopped. Friends and colleagues may try to help them consider other options, but their over-thinking only focuses on the one idea on their plate. They may even sacrifice great products, or services, that they already do well in their pursuit of the new celestial target.

When you watch a rocket zoom off, it looks spectacular as it climbs effortlessly into the sky. Then it explodes with a dazzle and is gone in a blink. The little stick falls to earth and either hits you on the head, or spears some poor little furry animal out collecting grubs and generally minding its own business.

Rockets tend to give you an excited stare and say, 'This is the one for me. I'm going to let everything else go and focus on this.'

One rocket I knew did really well to build up her

advertising business, and was then seduced by a slippery entrepreneur who whispered tender promises into her ear. She would be self-employed, but would run his web of businesses for him, as a senior partner. Fixed on this dream she chucked away all her existing customers and doggedly pursued the new goal, despite the warnings of her friends who couldn't see why this particular person really needed her. 'You're wrong,' she told them confidently. 'He has explained it all and it's fool-proof.' Six months later they had parted company and she was back on her own, without her customers. The entrepreneur had simply sucked up her connections and then engineered a brisk business divorce. Such is the danger for rockets when they meet fountains and are seduced by the promise of a glittering future.

If rocket-man is your middle name, be wary of gilt-edged opportunities. Think about other options and the downside to your new, brilliant project. Otherwise your stick could fall back to earth and skewer someone you love.

The sensible behaviour is to *balance* thinking with activity. Avoid hyper-thinking and do enough with your brain to get a reasonable, informed answer. Avoid hyper-activity and pace yourself, so that new information can be taken on board and course corrections made. Plenty of racing drivers get killed by ploughing into a wall at 200 mph. If they drove slower, they might lose the race, but they might also live. In business you need to live.

On the Firework Model of Stress, learn to perch on the centre cross, and make sure that you have just enough thinking to be useful and just enough activity to bring results, without burning yourself out too quickly. This is the 'sweet spot' where success flows from. If you wobble and step into one of the four quadrants, then jump out, dust yourself off and resume your perch, older, wiser and 10 times more alert.

Please turn to your Personal Planning Kit, section 3, called 'The Fireworks Code' (on page 163) and note down which firework best represents you. No cheating here. You might wish to check your answer with your partner, who will know you better than you know yourself.

So having worked out that I am a card-carrying catherine wheel, it was time for me to book my second appointment with myself. I showered, shaved and put on my smartest psychological suit. I was taking no chances.

Maun
Welcome back, my boy. Nice to see you again.
Me
Thank you. It's good to be here.
Maun
How did you get on with the fireworks? Any good?
Me
Interesting, but can't you just give me the job? I mean, I am family!
Maun
Don't be cheeky. We need to be sure you're up for it. The key thing is to be aware of your style and then you'll stand more chance of success.
Me
OK then. I'm a bit of a catherine wheel.
Maun
No, you're a *lot* of a catherine wheel. You can be a right pain sometimes. I should know, I have to live with you.
Me
Hmm... You're not making this easy, are you? (*Thinks.*) OK,

I'll keep an eye on myself and will remind myself that I can stop when I feel something is good enough.

Maun

Good. Any questions?

Me

Yes. What will my salary be?

Maun

Oh that's very funny! Ha ha ha, ho ho ho! Salary – yes, I like that! Any more?

Me

Yes... um, holiday entitlement?

Maun

Of course. Not.

Me

Pension?

Maun

Nichts.

Me

Sick pay?

Maun

Nada.

Me

So my benefit package is ...

Maun

Shit all. Comprenez-vous?

Me

OK, OK, I get the picture. I do have one question, though.

Maun

What's that?

Me

When can I start?

Maun

You already have! Welcome aboard. We love you!

Me
(*Beaming*) Thank you. What do I need to do first?
Maun
Oh, that's easy. Assemble your supporters' club, and then get on with selling.
Me
I thought accounts would come first?
Maun
Good God no, that's far too dull! We'll leave that to the end. Supporters first, then selling. If you can't sell then you'll go bust, and we can't have that.
Me
Ah! So you're one of my supporters then?
Maun
Well done, my boy. You'll go far. You're learning at last!
Me
Thank you. And one more thing ...
Maun
Yes?
Me
Don't call me boy!

Form Your Club

Round up your supporters

4

When you start off on your own, you are like a little chick, newly hatched into the world of foxes, bird flu and roast dinners. You may have been a hot-shot on your previous patch; you may come bristling with degrees, perhaps even an MBA. All of this effectively counts for nothing. When you are just out of the shell you can easily fall prey to your own chicky weaknesses. Working for yourself is a great leveller, like having children, or watching your team get thrashed on a wet Saturday afternoon. If you're starting at the bottom your gaze is upwards, so who do you look up to?

A good tip in business is to keep your hands in your pockets and your wallet at home. That way you can avoid getting into mischief and buying things you don't need. However, invest in a few beers with your supporters and it will pay dividends.

I lined up five people who all had something to offer me by way of support, advice, mentoring, or just being there to listen to my thinking and answer my dumb questions. Dumb questions are the best, because they are the ones you really want answered. Ask loads of them.

Think about who could help you. The list should include at least one person who is already doing what you do, as

Go through your address book and make a list of all the people you trust to give you sound advice, or who could open doors for you. Then whittle your list down to five top superstars, to keep things manageable. Once you have them lined up, turn to the Personal Planning Kit, to section 4 called 'Your Supporters Club' (on page 164) and write in their details, in order to have them in one handy place.

these people can give you a perspective based on their experiences. You can then check out some of your assumptions and reduce the risk of an early bath.

Compiling my supporters list was one of the best things I did when starting out on my own. One by one, I called my gang, visited them, bought them beer and asked them all my questions. They listened patiently and gave me great chunks of useful information and a strong sense that I was capable of being as successful as them. If you feel lonely or stuck, go out and spend time with your supporters and let them lift you up a bit. It worked for me.

The cost? Essentially nothing. The value? Essentially priceless. I learned that I could make money, that I would have to broaden my product portfolio, that finances were easy on day one, that selling could be mastered and that I was not going round the bend on some half-baked scheme. I even phoned a few more friends to double-check my scores on the insane-to-genius scale, and they all cooed comforting things down the telephone at me.

In my experience, friends will usually give you straight feedback. They may not say, 'You're a loser for thinking like that,' but if they don't think you're up to much they will find a way of getting their message across, perhaps by cutting your dream in half with a pointed question:

Are you *really* sure this is the right time to do this?

The best information is always hidden behind great questions, and we need to dream up some of our own to fling at our supporters. Think about all the things that are on your mind, which whirl around like so much space debris and keep you awake at night. All questions have value, and the most dangerous questions are the ones you don't ask. It's OK not to know things, because we're all allowed to have gaps in our knowledge.

> The fifth section of the Personal Planning Kit is called 'Team Questions' (on page 166). There are five questions there to get you started. Please think about what you want to know and add another five. Jot down more if you have more. If in doubt, go for quantity and not quality, as you could spend an age thinking of a great question, just to miss all the little obvious ones!

Once you have built your supporters club and answered your initial questions about
  'What if ...?' and
  'Could I ...?' and
  'When do I need to ...?' and
  'How much could I ...?'
you need to park your modesty in the basement of your ego and work out what you are good at. This is an essential step to take when you *are* your business.

People only buy from people they trust, and they seem to trust people who have a good sense of their own skills and talents. This level of self-awareness and confidence is reassuring and necessary because potential customers generally hate taking risks. When you get asked by friends, family and clients, 'Why do you work for yourself?' it pays to smile and to reply with a flourish that:
  'I was best electrical fitter in my year,' or
  'I love being a painter,' or
  'I'm confident my website will be the next big thing,' or
  'I'm passionate about flowers,' or even
  'Consultancy really makes my nipples go hard!'

I noticed that my best days and happiest times at work happened when I was coaching people. Having parked my own modesty some years ago, I would admit to being a quick learner, good at working with people and able to generate options for clients out of thin air. It's taken me a while to say these things out loud, and I've noticed that people do respond well when you talk positively about yourself.

So the core questions are:

What do you do well?

What do you better than your competitors?

We are all unique, and we all have our own combination of skills and talents. Even being a good all-rounder can be special when pitted against someone who has a combination of polarized expertise and a whacking great blind spot.

In the world of selling, small differences can have big impacts, if you notice them. So stand back from yourself and take a look. What little gems are tucked into the folds of your personality? What rubies lurk there to show people?

Being modest is not going to win many customers because people don't want to go into an average tea shop and eat bland cake. They want hot fresh coffee and a deliciously moist almond slice with a sensuous strawberry filling. If you were on your own menu, would you get eaten?

For example, if you are a good designer, say so and enjoy telling people. Be proud of your portfolio and talk with passion about what you really enjoy doing. If you go large on these things, your business will flourish. Think of it as emotional working capital. If you have none, you're going straight to hell for an eternity of greasy fish and chips, washed down with firewater from the spitting lakes of lava. And that will just give you indigestion.

Pause here and think about what skills you have and what talents you will bring to your business. Adding skills and experiences together can be a great way to give yourself an edge, as you will be the only one with that specific combination.

When you have some answers, turn to section 6 of the Personal Planning Kit, called 'I am Special Because ...' (on page 167), and sketch in some examples of the strengths and talents that will help to make you and your business a success.

So now you have assembled a supporters club and thought about your strengths, it's time to leave the safety of the tea shop and head out into the high street. You need to join the real world and keep your feet while struggling against the tide of Saturday shoppers, all rushing to catch the bus home.

Unless you are good at the subject the next chapter introduces you to, your self-employed life will probably be short, rough and expensive. There might be tears before bedtime, but you have to take the risk. Time to turn over the page and find out about the most important skill needed to be successful.

Listen Please

Sales secrets for beginners

5

Selling Part One: The Lesson About Ears

To work for yourself and be successful does not mean that you have to be a slick salesperson, with more patter than a litter of kittens. It does not mean that you have to develop an oily handshake and a greasy smile. And it does not mean that you have to change your name to Gavin and wear a chunky bracelet with your name on it, in case you forget who you are.

The bad news is that you *will* have to sell to people, because if you don't, you wont have a business. You may need to sell your idea to the bank manager to raise some funds; you may have to sell it to your partner to secure his or her emotional support. You may even have to sell it to yourself, to convince yourself that your hare-brained scheme really does have more chance of success than England does of winning football's World Cup again.

If you are tempted to sidestep this chapter because either:

- You can get by on massive ego alone, or
- You already have a successful sales background, or
- You don't intend to succeed

then please think again, because help is at hand. Selling does not have to be complicated, or false, or insincere. Wrapped into the mix is also a selling secret that a surprisingly large number of people, most of them professional salespeople, skip past.

The secret of selling is – um, let's come back to that later on in the book.

I'll be honest here and say that I am not the best salesperson in the world, but I *am* the best person to sell my services to others. A friend of mine was running a business which was struggling to find new customers, and he made the cardinal mistake of employing a salesperson to go and get them. This was silly for several reasons, one of which was that it made a massive dent in his cashflow when he could least afford it. Also there is often a six-month time lag between hiring sales-people and their starting to bring in business, so you are adding six months of salary to your working capital. Of course the salesperson might fail to earn a bean, and then you've gambled away your cash. It happens.

The best option is for you to sell your products, because you know your business and are more passionate about it than anyone else can hope to be. The person my friend hired had good credentials – he was a salesman, after all – and could sell himself very well. Trouble was, he was useless at selling corporate training services, and my friend learned a very expensive and time-consuming lesson.

If you want to be dazzled with the A-to-Z of selling, please go and buy a book on the subject, because here we are only going to have a gentle snuffle through the key bits. We shall think about marketing later on, a subject which can veer towards the soap-bubble end of intellectual rigour, but compared with this, selling is your wig-wearing bald coot of a brute at the management top table. A hard case with 'win' tattooed across his knuckles. However, if you want to make it to the end of your first trading year, then stick on that head rug and listen up.

The best sales lesson I ever learned happened in a crowded and steamy roadside café. It was the sort of place where the sausages were more qualified than the serving staff, and whose reputation for 'home-cooked food' suffered a dent when one of the Neanderthal chefs idly commented to a visiting journalist, one deep-fried Thursday, that she couldn't have an omelette because they hadn't been delivered yet. However these places can be the backbone of a wandering selfer's life, and you may wish to swallow your *haute cuisine* principles and make friends with your local travel café. They're warm, free to use and handily placed for meeting people. Just avoid the food.

Anyway I was sitting at a tired wooden table, facing my own business coach, a genial fellow by the name of Harry. Mrs Thatcher, the much beloved and much reviled first female prime minister, was once famously quoted as saying, 'Every prime minister needs a Willie.' She was not, as it happened, referring to her possible status as a pre-op transvestite, but rather was commenting on Willie Whitelaw, her famously ever-present adviser. In this way I would suggest that everybody needs a Harry. He is my business coach, and is there to straighten me out when I get crumpled, and to top up my business teacup when it runs dry. Some people seem surprised that I have a business coach, but there is no need to be. Nobody is born with all-round business acumen. Look closely at the top dudes and they all have advisers lurking in the shadows.

So there I was, facing Harry and about to run through my sales pitch for the first time. The place was packed, the waiting staff avoiding the customers and the customers avoiding the omelettes. I had been up until two in the morning producing a magnificent pitch, in true catherine-wheel style, and my eyes felt sore and gritty. In one hand I gripped a bulky 'welcome pack', to introduce my business, and in the other I gripped a printout of my 10-minute, 10-slide presentation. Suited and booted for good measure, I was taking no chances and the stage was set for my moment of triumph. Harry had agreed that we would treat the exercise as a genuine meeting, and was now poised and expectant, his eyes watching me with interest.

'Good morning Harry,' I began earnestly, in my politest

tones, 'and thank you for seeing me today. I would like to start by running through a short presentation, and then I will take you through the welcome pack, all of which will last no more than 20 minutes.' I felt my adrenalin surge and lift me. This was going to be easy.

Harry leaned forwards. The corners of his mouth twitched and a small but discernible cloud scudded across his brow. 'Would you like me to make a comment now, or shall I save it until you've finished?' he asked in a genial way, but with the unmistakable force of a steel tent peg being casually shoved into a party balloon.

'Leave it to the end,' I croaked through tight lips, my heart flopping about with worry. My adrenalin was now pooling on the floor.

'Fair enough then, Richard. Do carry on,' he smiled generously, but it was too late. What was his comment? I had asked him to give me feedback, but doing so a mere 10 seconds into my impressively constructed and minutely detailed presentation was surely taking the piss? I sailed on, but my heart was now comatose and my tiredness returned. Twenty minutes later Harry nodded wisely and then gave me a piece of advice which had clearly been on his mind for at least 19 minutes and 50 seconds. 'The art of selling,' he said in deep, polished and not unfriendly tones, 'is to *listen.*'

So, sitting there in my suit and with my bits of paper, hot and sweaty and being eyed by a clump of fly-specked waiting staff, I learned my lesson.

Shut up. Shut up and listen.

Listen or don't bother selling. Indeed it shouldn't really even be called 'selling', it should be called 'listening', and we should hire listenpeople instead of salespeople. If we did that, the world would be a better place and we would look forward to the next sales visit from some footsore door-knocker as it would give us a chance to be listened to.

'People really like it when they are talking,' Harry continued, smoothly ice-skating his way to more sales gems, 'they really do. They feel good about themselves. So, instead of you talking, your job is to get me talking. Then you can listen out for my problems and needs, and then' – he paused, just because he has the sort of voice that needs a few good pauses for the listener to fully appreciate his resonant timbre – 'and then you can answer those needs with the products or services your business supplies. It's as simple as that.'

I nodded, like a child who has just learned that one plus one is two, and who feels a bit stupid for not realizing this before. Out of the corner of my eye I could have sworn that I saw some people hovering near the next table, nodding at me as if to say, 'Stupid prick. Even we knew that and we're just fly-specked waiting staff.'

After this humbling experience I ditched my slides and my ostentatious 'welcome pack' and made sure that I had a couple of really informative leaflets in my briefcase. Two weeks later I made a sales call to a friend who ran a PR business. He was a good chap and knew I was starting out as a selfer, so was happy to see me. Just as I parked and switched off the car's ignition, I was struck hard by a thought. He wasn't my friend. He was a businessman whom I knew. Big difference. He wasn't seeing me to be nice, he was seeing me because I might be of use to him, and therefore he would treat me in the same way as he would any other rep coming in to waste his time, drink his coffee and clutter up his office – that is, with bored disdain.

Sitting in his meeting room we exchanged a few pleasantries about the weather and the likelihood of rain, then he said, 'So, Richard, what's your business all about?'

Avoiding the obvious waffle-trap, I countered with, 'Coaching and profiling and personal development work, but as we haven't met for a while I'm interested to know more about your business. How many people do you have working for you now?'

I then listened to him for half an hour, and was able to link some of his concerns about one of his new starters to the usefulness of coaching. We had a productive conversation. Although he didn't buy anything from me, he had given me a great opportunity to practise my listening skills, which is easily done if you ask questions. When I left the meeting I knew that I had cracked it, and stopped on the way home to buy a take-out Chinese dinner. I also bought a take-out Thai dinner (I was fairly pleased with myself) and was promptly given a tough time by my wife for spending more money than was necessary. She was right, and it never hurts to be reminded that the best place for your money is in your pocket and not someone else's.

Rubbish salespeople drone on about their products; great salespeople ask you questions to get you talking. You then feel good about yourself, and are more receptive when they magically answer a need you have just expressed. 'Wow!' You will find yourself replying, 'that's amazing! Because I was wondering where I could buy a Sugar Lump 2000 personal computer, complete with a rough-rider mouse and a handsomely proportioned microphone for oral pleasure over the internet.' And the sales-whiz will smile and know he has done a great job of listening.

For reasons unknown to science, florists tend to provide free master classes in selling. Perhaps this is because they are used to dealing with ignorant blokey types, like me, who think that Flowers is just a type of beer. Usually I creep nervously into the local petal palace and try to look confident. Usually I fail.

'I'd like to buy some flowers please,' is my cunningly vague opening gambit.

Instead of replying, 'Here, take these,' the florist complicates matters considerably by being helpful and asking, 'What sort of flowers would you like?'

'White ones', I tend to reply, trying to avoid her fiendish mind games.

'Would you like some lilies?'

'No thanks, I want white flowers.'

'Lilies are white.'

'Then I would like some lilies, please. What do they look like?'

'Like this.'

'Oh! So that's a lily, is it!' (I am now an expert in one flower.)

Then having established a sales bridgehead, the florist breaks out and goes rumbling into the low countries for ultimate victory, by asking a range of supplementary questions, to do with packaging, ribbons, weird green foliage and whether I would like a card. All of this means I have to think about what I want. However, the end result of the surgically precise flower power quiz is that I feel well serviced, and come away with a lighter wallet, but a deeper sense of security than when I ambled in. I feel looked after.

Spend time asking questions, and only when you have made the other party feel good by listening to him or her can you offer a couple of options from your portfolio. Never just bang the answer on the table, as it can make people feel either stupid, for not knowing it already, or resentful at having something thrust at them against their will.

People love choice, so give your potential customers a choice, and they will feel part of the process and forget that they are being sold to. One of the choices might seem worthless to you, but that's not the point. The point is that they will be leading the decision making, and of course will be making the decision for themselves, which is the best way to get the decision to stick. Your job is simply to listen, offer a choice, outline what differentiates you from the competition, and then let nature take its course. This isn't manipulation and it's not insincerity. It's simply a great way to talk to people and a great way to earn income, which builds cashflow.

People buy people. It's been said before and it's worth repeating. If they like the look of you and you listen well, they might buy from you. If you look like a bank robber, or leave mud on their carpet, they won't.

Years ago I was looking for a house to rent while working away from home. I had slogged round the local area, to which I was new, and had seen a number of over-priced flats and houses which I wouldn't have let to a cat. My last appointment was to see a clean bungalow in a street dominated by retired folk. The joke was that residents arrived in a removal van and left in an ambulance, which later turned out to be only slightly untrue. The estate agent looked at me with pity in her eyes, and said, with a heavy sigh that she was keen to see the place go, but that it was owned by an old lady who lived next door and who hated people. In particular she hated young men, and had sent a number of them packing.

'No problem,' I said, with my friendliest young-man smile, 'I'll get on with her.' Then, before I rang the doorbell for the appointment, I had a brainwave and phoned my wife. 'Quick question dear,' I said. 'How do you charm old ladies?' She thought for a minute and then replied, 'Be nice to them. Talk about flowers. They like flowers.'

Shit. Not my best subject. I only do lilies.

After I had smiled my way through the introduction, my potential landlady escorted me next door to her spare bungalow. I spied some rose bushes growing in the front garden. Aha! Salvation! We used to have rose bushes when I was a kid, and the buggers always tried to reach out and scratch you as you walked past.

'Lovely roses,' I purred. 'I do like flowers. Did you have to work hard to get them this looking this good?'

The old witch stopped looking at me as if I was about to mug her and smiled. 'Not really,' she said with pride, 'but I do water them every day.'

After that it was plain sailing. I charmed my way round two bedrooms, a bathroom, a small kitchen and a shed, admiring the furniture and the décor as each door was opened. I rented the property, which was a great place to live, paid my bills on time, and even did a deal with her to buy the television set when we swapped her furniture for ours.

Now you might think I was being cheeky, but if you want to sell yourself to people it pays to take an interest in them. When the estate agent handed me the keys she was surprised that I had secured the property, and happily told me that the landlady was insistent that it be rented to that 'nice young man'.

Such is the way of sales. You just need to find something to be interested in, ask simple questions, listen to the answers and then give people a choice. In my case, for the old lady, the choice was that I paid full rent or that she gave me a discount. She opted for the full whack, but by then I was in. Hooray!

The skill with asking good questions is to ask ones that help potential customers reveal the features and benefits they need from your products, which you can then deliver up to them. At a basic level, just get them talking. A good opener is simply:

Tell me about your business?

This is usefully vague, and invites people to tell you all sorts of things. If they waffle on, just indulge them. You can always ask sharper follow-up questions, such as:

- How many people work for you?
- What issues do you have that you would like to resolve?
- What training needs to do you currently have?
- Which features of this product are more important to you?
- What occasion are the flowers for?

The question about training needs is clearly aimed at me selling training workshops. If potential clients reply 'none', I show them a leaflet and ask, 'If you had a need, which option would it most likely be for?' That keeps the conversation moving. Sometimes I ask about the ordering process, as I need to check that I am in fact sitting in front of the right person. Plenty of people have sat in front of a personnel manager trying to flog training, only to be told that none is needed, when around the corner in the same building an operational manager is tearing her hair out at the lack of communication skills, and wondering why nobody ever gets trained.

Make sure you are sitting in front of the decision maker and have not been fobbed off with a bored junior, who has been despatched to keep you warm for a few minutes before spitting you out into the winter snow.

There are two basic question types to play with, open and closed. Both have value, and both sorts can be used to shepherd the sales conversation into a little wooden sheep-pen.

Closed questions are ones that can only be answered with a 'yes' or 'no' or with a choice, such as 'How do you like your steak? Crisped, medium, or so blue it has an x-certificate?' These are useful for closing down avenues of exploration, or for establishing a definite answer.

Open questions elicit a general answer, and encourage people to think. Damp squibs and fountains may have problems answering these, given that thinking is not their strong point, so if they block your question with an answer that does not relate to it, simply smile and say, 'That's interesting. Who would have thought the floods of '66 would have caused so much damage! Now I wonder if you could tell me which style of uPVC conservatory you most prefer?'

If you get stuck, a tip to remember is this. Closed questions tend to begin with

'Do you ...?'

while open questions tend to begin with

'What do you ...?',

'How do you ...',

'When would you ...?',

'What sort?',

'How many?',

'Where will you ...?'

and so on. The person answering them has to think for a moment, before revealing some useful information to you.

Practise asking questions around the home with your family, or down the pub with your friends. Get into the habit of asking them and then sitting patiently, smiling through the answer. Then turn to your Personal Planning Kit, to section 7, called 'Creating an Opening' (on page 168), and note down three questions that will help you to find out a 'need' you can address.

Harry advised me that when calling to make an appointment, I should ask for only half an hour and go for a point just before lunch, as that is when people tend to be near their office and can squeeze in some time. Most people can fit a quick 30 minutes into their day, so your pitch is designed *only* to get to see them. Like a boiled toffee, selling doesn't like to be hurried. An easy pace wins more customers than a desperate 'buy now' plea.

I have used this tactic on a number of occasions and it has always delivered results. Sometimes I've had a useful 30 minutes and then booked a second meeting to discuss things in more detail. Other times the potential customer has been happy to overrun (always a good sign) and we have chatted on.

Overrunning, asking you questions, fiddling with your samples, taking leaflets and talking about costs are known as buying signals. Watch out for them and log them when they occur, as they can help you to work out how well the meeting is going.

Lots of people, in my experience, are frightened by ringing up to make an appointment, but there is no need to be. Accept the fact that you will get rejected many times. They are not rejecting *you*, because they don't know you. They are rejecting what they think you are offering, and you remain, as ever, a happy whole person. I have coached a few people round this issue of avoiding 'cold calling', as they like to call it, and have discovered there are two key ways to keep sane.

The first is that when the other person answers the telephone, ask them if they have a minute to talk, and if not, book a time with the person later in the day. This avoids them feeling hassled, and it respects the fact that they are likely to be busy. When you do get to talk, state your case in a minute (which we shall cover in a subsequent chapter) and then end by asking an open question, such as 'Tell me something about your business?' At the end of the conversation, use a classic closed question to move to an appointment, such as 'What times do you prefer, morning or afternoon?'

The second point is to not call it 'cold calling'. Instead call it 'cold listening'. This approach helped a consultant to overcome his fear, because listening is a non-threatening entity. Your job is then simply to ring up, ask a couple of open questions and listen to the answers. Try it; it can work for you. With this simple change my consultant colleague has now chalked up a number of sales successes.

Selling Part Two: The Bit About Numbers

Selling is also a numbers game, so we'll take a pass at some numbers here, numbers which any self-respecting selfer needs to know. If you don't do your maths you are highly likely to trip and fall, and spend a small bag of groats with your accountant, just for him to tell you that 'Yes, you have gone bust.'

When I began my business, once I had pulled myself out of catherine-wheel mode and got active, I filled my diary each week with visits. It didn't matter if I drove 200 miles for a half-hour appointment. That was still 100 per cent more useful than sitting at home.

Generally speaking 95 per cent of all selling effort is wasted, but only hindsight can tell you which is your happy 5 per cent. Then you can refine the customers you are targeting, although effort and more effort is needed.

Think about it. If you could get a hit rate of 50 per cent everybody would set up in business – if it was *that* easy, and it isn't.

In order to decide what you will be selling, every business

needs a sales forecast, and every forecast is really just a bad guess written down, but at least it's better than a wet finger up your backside. When compiling your rubbish guesses – sorry, forecasts – remember that it can take up to six months to make a sale, for a consultancy job, corporate training work or interim management project. The process of introducing yourself, having a first meeting, having a second meeting, waiting for a decision and then actually doing the work can easy slip and slide through a whole half year. Then you may need to wait two months for your money, so it doesn't take a room full of PhD students to work out why lots of consultancy businesses can go bust dead quick. They over-estimate the speed and size of their sales successes, and run out of cash, while muttering to themselves that next month will be the biggie that sets everything right.

It won't.

It never goes like this, unless you're in Hollywood. Selling is a slow process, and if your estimates are not cautious, your business moth will soon burn itself to a frazzle on the glowing light bulb of insane over-optimism.

Selling bacon rolls does not require six months to get going, or you would be sitting on bacon chairs and sleeping in a bacon bed. However, don't assume that because your product is simpler, you will be slicing and serving a pig a week from the word go. It will take time to find loyal customers and to ramp up your output. Be conservative with your guesses, and work hard to sell to a wide range of people.

Whilst I was planning my self-employed life, I worked out how much I needed to earn each month to cover my costs, and divided this by my daily fee rate to find out how many days I needed to work. The first number I arrived at was slightly more days than the average month actually contains, which was a bit of a bugger.

I was then advised by a consultant friend that lots of people doing this kind of work tend to invoice every other day on average, the rest being taken up by selling and admin activities. This meant that I would only have *half* the capacity I thought I had in order to make hay, which meant that I needed to *double* my daily fee rate to recover enough income to pay the bills. Not only was this a massive shock, but it reinforced the need to really know your business numbers. If you don't, you could find yourself selling £10 notes for £9.00, and even boy scouts aren't that slow.

For consultant types the 'half time' equation seems to work out. Excluding weekends and bank holidays, there is a maximum of 253 invoiceable days in any given year. Assuming you will actually book work for half this amount, the total we quickly get to is 125 chargeable days. (If you want to argue about odd days here, then you have a problem, you catherine-wheel you.) Given that 125 days is now 100 per cent of your capacity it's foolish to base your calculations on such a high booking rate. Better to go for something realistic such as 80 per cent, which gives a figure of 100 days in which to make enough money to pay all the bills.

However, a quick way to work out your daily fee rate is to take your existing salary and trim off the last two noughts. For people earning £30,000 a year and wishing to set themselves up as consultant types, their daily fee rate needs to be around £300 to return roughly the same level of income. Multiply it by 100 days to get back to your original salary if you want to work in both directions.

Know your numbers so you know at what level to pitch yourself. Add to this the fabulous differentiating factors you will be dreaming up in the next chapter, and stir in your effortless questioning technique, and there is no need to sell on price. If you do, you just leave yourself exposed to the next person who will come along and undercut you. Value yourself, and if you feel your rate is fair and justifiable (which it is), stick with it.

A colleague of mine was aghast when we were discussing rates and we discovered that mine was over double hers. She asked me, her eyes wide with disbelief, 'But what happens when people can't afford your rate?' 'Simple,' I replied with a grin. 'I don't work for them.'

Despite my bullish pricing policy I will vary my price a bit if I really want to work for someone and they simply don't have the funds available, such as a charity. I'm also aware though, that if you drop the price too low, people are suspicious that there must be something wrong for it to be *that* cheap.

Conversely, people are happy to pay more if they perceive good service comes with the package, or there is a sense of exclusivity. People buy from florists because they have choice and service. If their buying decision was based solely on price, all flowers would be picked up from the local supermarket or garage forecourt.

Think about all the things you have stuffed into your shopping bags over the last month. How many of them were the cheapest of their kind? How many of them had the right brand name stitched into the seam?

The internet hasn't quite wiped out our vast shopping malls yet, although it's well on the way to doing more for our industrial landscape than global warming is. Despite the high-tech advances, people still buy from places they trust, and Amazon's business philosophy is simply 'we deliver'. Nobody is going to buy cheaply if the goods fail to turn up and you don't need too many delivery failures to cause your shiny new web-shop to implode. Amazon's philosophy underpins its whole business success, and it means that people buy on a combination of price and service and not just price alone.

Scarcity, or lack of it, can have a big impact on the price you charge. A local bistro I visited charged £15 for a lunchtime meal, when across the road its competition only charged £10. Both were equal in terms of quality and service, so the bistro lost out and soon had to reduce its prices. There was no shortage of good-quality food on offer, so *abundance* helped to fix the selling price.

A close friend of mine used to work as a Saturday boy, selling electrical goodies to the unwary. The wily manager who employed him knew all about scarcity. On one particularly grey and drizzly day, just before closing time, a damp and worried-looking customer burst into the shop waving a lump of mangled metal.

'Do you have a spare washing machine motor to replace this?' he asked anxiously.

The manager took the lump and examined it carefully. 'Yes, sir. We do, sir,' the manager informed him politely. 'We have one left.'

'Oh, great! Thank you,' replied the happy customer, with evident relief. 'How much is it?'

'£100,' replied the manager.

'What? But they're only £50 down the road at the discount warehouse!'

'And do they have any in stock?'

'No.'

'Well then,' the manager smiled, 'when they have some and we don't, we only charge £50 as well.'

Selling is about asking questions, listening for opportunities and meeting people's needs. It all begins with knowing your numbers, so that you know where to set your price. If you need help with maths then see your accountant, because that is his speciality. Yours is to be a star, in whatever field you choose.

Selling does not have to be difficult, but people make it hard for themselves by either knowing nothing about it or

> Please turn to section 8 of your Personal Planning Kit,
> called 'Selling by Numbers (on page 169). Think
> about the prices you will charge and the volumes you
> will sell, and have fun wrestling with your sales fore-
> cast. Then trim it to 80 per cent of your capacity to
> make life harder and therefore more realistic for you.

saying, 'I couldn't do that.' I have fallen into both camps,
and now realize that I could have done a bit better to begin
with, had I not been quite so scared. When it goes well it's
great fun, and now even I look forward to meeting potential
customers and having the chance to listen to their story.

It's OK to be nervous and to book a couple of easy sales
meetings to cut your teeth, or to invite a friend to help in
your shop for a couple of days. It's also OK to have had no
prior experience and to peddle hard to make a success of
your business. Working for myself has improved my selling
skills by at least 300 per cent, which is the minimum
number I needed to improve by, in order to avoid starving.
If I can do it, anyone can do it. There's no magic in it, just
a few basic principles and dogged slog.

So now we're fully armed with a battery of useful
numbers and two large well-trained ears, we can move on to
the perennial question of:

But what do I actually say to secure a sale?

To answer this question we shall look at three things, over the
next three chapters: marketing, the big secret and contracting
for success. However, before we get to our sumptuous feast of
usefulness, there are two small *hors d'oeuvres* to wrap our
tongue round and savour. Here they are:

One: A big selling mistake that lots of people make is to
forget to ask for the order. If you don't ask, then the
answer is always no!

Two: Remember also that the old sales sweats pounding
the motorways in their climate-controlled mobile
homes have the following engraved on their heart:

A sale is never really a sale until the money is in the
bank.

Be Different or Be Dead

The essence of marketing

6

Every business has a personality. Some of them are like cunning little foxes which weave in and out of the market place with the stealth of a sharp-toothed guided missile. Others are well-established moo-cows who plod around chewing the grass, and who generally get by because of their size and unthreatening appearance. Still more are like bees that flit between the brightly coloured flowers, sucking up a tasty squirt of nectar and leaving the foxes and cows to their own territories. Others are like rats which gnaw away at the work created by others, generally adding little to the existing market place and occasionally leaving behind a virulent disease.

Rat businesses are synonymous with bad debts and a crushing lack of goodwill, in the same way that the Black Death wiped out a third of the population of Great Britain between 1348 and 1350. On the plus side, it did bring about the end of the feudal system and helped to emancipate the peasants. This was great news for the one in three who survived, but a bastard for the two in three who did not.

If your business lived in the countryside, would it be a cow, a fox, a bee or a rat? Would it have whiskers or wings? Would it be colourful or black and white? To be successful and to make your success stick you need to think about what makes you different, which means messing about with *marketing*. And we will start by chuckling over that well-worn marketing quote:

> Half of all money spent on marketing is wasted. The trick is knowing which half.

Some people say that 'marketing' is the most important thing to get right in a business, and that it's vital to be an expert in this field. The people who say this also happen to be marketing professionals themselves, which is a suspicious coincidence. I worked for a manager once whose view was that 'marketing' was something only worth considering on a Friday afternoon, when the important work of the week was done and he was lounging around chewing the fat with his team.

In a curious way he was right. If you let marketing go to your head it can take over your business, and you can spend the gross domestic product of some dusty foreign country on advertising, brochures and free chunky pens.

On the other hand he was dead wrong. Marketing is worth spending some quality time on because it can help to bring you new customers, increase the value of your product and defend your business from aggressive competition. Marketing is the language you use to speak to customers with. Just like the way we communicate in everyday life, marketing is a combination of what you say, how you say it and whether your delivery is heard by the customers you are targeting.

I used to think that people who did marketing were all a bunch of pretentious fops, who had a first degree in wearing loud shirts and a Master's in obnoxious and boorish behaviour. Their lives were a tangle of pubs, clubs and creative marketing meetings, where they argued passionately about which shade of the colour blue would best represent the brand value, and whether their expense account was sufficiently intimating enough to earn them a promotion to Chief Swank. However, a handful of years ago I discovered two things which opened my eyes to my prejudices. One was that business-to-business marketing did not have to be hot air and hogwash; it could be useful and could genuinely help a business to develop.

The second thing was a book by Theodore Levitt, called *The Marketing Imagination*.[3] Normally the only books I

---

3 Published by the Free Press, 1986.

recommend are my own, and given that bookselling is a more cut-throat business than high seas piracy, this is a perfectly reasonable strategy. In this case I shall make an exception because the book contains one of the wisest bits of business advice that I have ever read. We shall ponder it here. For me it sums up all the good things about marketing, which needs to be separated from marketing people, who are to serious thought what alcopops are to the Campaign for Real Ale.

The fourth chapter of my copy of Theo's tome is sagely titled 'Differentiation – of anything'. It starts by saying:

> There is no such thing as a commodity. All goods and services can be differentiated and usually are. Though the usual presumption is that this is true more of consumer goods than of industrial goods and services, the opposite is the actual case.

Differentiate or die is my marketing motto, and it has served me well. The way I have run my own business, and handled marketing work when producing simple business-to-business trade advertising and brochures, has been to make what I do look slightly different from my competitors.

Marketing is about getting your message across to the people you want to bag as customers, and if your message is the same as the next person's, then it is harder for people to decide in your favour. Therefore, the more clear water you put between your products or services and those of the competition, the easier it is for people to choose you. And the bonus here is your don't need a qualification in marketing to do this, or own a shirt that would make a bird of paradise look like a dumpy old chicken.

One summer we needed our cooker fixing, something I would probably kill myself doing if I tried to mess with a cocktail of gas and electricity. The cooker man turned up on time and soon cured the fault. He cleared up after himself and was polite and helpful. When I asked about the cost of the work he said '£49.00' and was instantly provided with a cheque for that amount.

He could have had a cheque for £55.00, but he didn't ask for it. Keeping his cost a whisker below the magic '50' had no impact for me, because we were not buying on price. We simply wanted someone to fix the fault speedily and without leaving a mess. In the grand scheme of things an extra £6.00 is neither here nor there when you have bacon to fry and no means of getting your breakfast. Our cooker man did the job well, we recommended him to friends and shall use him again ourselves.

The point of the story is that if he had differentiated himself clearly he could have asked for more money and could have avoided being overly cautious with his pricing. When multiplied by a year's worth of cooker fixing, this adds up to a big extra slab of spendable cash.

People do not always buy only on price, which is a message we have already encountered when thinking about selling, but it's worth repeating. Plenty of people buy the special offers at the local supermarket and then splash out on luxury items – wine and beer perhaps – which allows the same shop to maintain its profits quite easily. When I go to a supermarket I buy on location, cleanliness, the freshness of the fruit, the choice available and the speed and efficiency of the checkout staff. I have no idea how much my basket of goodies is going to cost me until the smiling lady on the till reads out a number, and I go a bit giddy in the head and mutter something about 'things only costing a few pence when I was a lad'. Personally I couldn't give a bee's kneecaps about the price of the products, because if I have less money I put fewer things in my basket; I don't actually go and buy cheaper stuff.

Just to demonstrate this point about price, put a price next to the following staples:

- A pint of full fat milk
- A loaf of granary bread
- A box of washing powder, to get your clothes so white people mistake you for an angel.

I have no idea myself, which is how I know that I'm not buying on price. Something else is informing my decision-making process: possibly flash packaging, or the promise of eternal youth if I eat the right kind of cheese. All these different facets of branding help me to tell the difference between two broadly similar products – and who wouldn't vote for eternal youth anyway?

Thus, to help get your message across to people you need to let them know what makes your business different. That gives them a whole shopping-basket load of reasons to buy from you and not from your competitor, whom they have cunningly lined up to meet five minutes after you have departed.

Businesses can market tangible products (cars, coffee, carpets) or they can market intangible products (coaching, counselling, computer advice). Businesses can mix and match these to produce uniqueness, which allows them to differentiate themselves from a rival and so help the potential customer to make a choice between the two.

Consider a hairdressing business. The tangible product is the haircut itself. You see your hair change and that is what you pay for, unless it turns orange by mistake instead of 'golden glowing summer sunset', which happened to a friend of mine. However, you may also choose your stylist because they offer smart premises with comfortable chairs and a decent cup of coffee, which is all part of the product offering and tangible reasons to choose them.

Some hairdressers stop there, but others add in additional layers of service to make sure you stick with them and don't desert to a cheesily named competitor. A decent conversation can be a great way to keep clients. A pleasant telephone manner when a client calls for an appointment is essential, as is a smile and a 'no problem' when the same client changes the booking. All of these are intangible – service – benefits, and in their own right each one may be enough of a reason for you to choose to go there.

If you have these things all lined up, customers rarely ask about the price, or mind if you are 50p more expensive than the rest of the hairdressing salons in your high street. Add up the number of haircuts you might do in a year, and if you don't want all those extra 50ps please post them to me and I'll spend them for you.

Names are the first point of differentiation. Think about all the pop bands who use weird or wacky names to make themselves stand out. Witty business names can easily date, can sound jaded, and may give the impression that you are in it for your own self-aggrandisement. Make sure you road-test your potential name first, before splashing it in massive letters on your work shirts.

When you have a list of possible names there are three places where you would be wise to go and check them out. The first is Companies House, to make sure there is not currently a limited company with the same name. The second place is the Patent Office, to check whether the name is an existing trademark. You may get sued if you tread on people's toes here. Finally, make sure the web address is available for your name. All these things can be checked over the internet, and if you pass all three 'tests' your name should last you and will not be confused with that of another business.

Take a minute to write out at least three different business names for your venture, then pop them in your Personal Planning Kit in section 9, called 'The Name Game' (on page 170).

When potential customers ask me how much I charge, I look them in the eye and tell them. Then without pausing I go on to mention several benefits of choosing me. Invariably they never ask about a price reduction because they want to discuss these added benefits. It's a bit like haggling over the type of 'free' car mats the garage will put into your new motor, when you have already swallowed the list price without a murmur.

People love tangible things such as free training handouts, and they also love the intangible things such as the warmth and passion in your voice and the impression they get from a well-cut business suit, or a clean set of overalls. Tell your customers what you do well, and what you do differently from the competition. They really want to know.

My own business is differentiated quite simply by me. There is no other business that features me and therefore it's unique. Realizing that I am never going to replace Keanu Reeves as a celluloid heart throb, I have to major on other aspects of being me in order to make a crust. All of these things enable me to get my message across and win business. I talk freely about my skills and experience and qualifications, because my combination is unique to me.

Coaching services can easily be seen as intangible, so I also talk about specific profiling tools and meeting primers and feedback sheets. Clients can touch them and look at them, and this helps to set me apart from those people who just talk about 'coaching' in its own right.

With me, you can buy the whole package – and even if you choose not to, the option is always there for you.

A big juicy, throbbing intangible benefit is that I am passionate about what I do. Not evangelical, just genuinely really keen on working alongside people. A number of people, when I asked, have said that they booked me because they 'just like the fact that you love your work'. After all, would you want to hire someone who was depressed?

We did once. It was a plumber who carried the troubles of the world on his shoulders, and although his work was perfectly acceptable he was easily displaced by a sunnier rival, who didn't carry his own stormcloud around with him.

In my experience of networking with small businesses and also facilitating personal development workshops, it never ceases to amaze me how reluctant people are to actually tell others what they do well, or what they do at all. Simply *telling* people what your business features and benefits are can be a differentiating factor. Incredible but true. If you don't tell 'em they don't know. Simple as that.

Pause a moment and consider why this is. It is not something generally listed in all the marketing books, which can dribble on about cash cows, profit panthers and hedge fund hedgehogs. Instead think about some of the rubbish our parents or guardians lashed into us. I know plenty of people who completely understand the need to market themselves, but who carry around some or all of the following leaden phrases in their head:

Self praise is no praise.

You don't blow your own trumpet.

Hide your light under a bushel. (What the hell is a bushel anyway?)

Talking about yourself is arrogant and is not something *nice* people do.

We are the air-cooled disc brakes on the level of business success we can achieve. So we need to think about our greatness and develop a business attitude that is not arrogant or deceitful, and that instead celebrates us and all the things our business does well and differently.

This is perfectly OK, and you can celebrate being you. Some of the stuff we sucked up as kids was well meant, but wasn't designed for the rough and tumble of working for yourself in business. You can be the best boss you ever had if you want to, so be kind to yourself and relish the things you consider to be your assets. Share them with friends, and savour the moment.

You can enjoy being you, and can erase some of the less useful messages that fill the dusty databanks in your head. Replace them with one or more of the following:

- You can know what you do well.
- You can share what you do well with new people.
- You can include your strengths in your marketing brochure.

- You can choose to celebrate your strengths.
- You can smile and be proud of yourself.

If you don't, then you run a high risk that you will just sell on price, and so reduce your net profit and positive cashflow. You will have to work twice as hard to keep ahead of the likes of me, who will aim to outpace you with a clearer marketing message that is chock full of tempting morsels to make the customer mine.

Before you think about yourself, a good way to study differentiation in the real world is to go and have lunch on two days in two similar places. Write down all the things that are different between them, such as:

- The décor.
- The crockery.
- Any house specialities.
- The style of the menu.
- The time taken to be served.
- The garnish on the plate.
- The comfort of the chairs.
- The cheery wave goodbye.

Notice how some of these differences are tiny. We do notice them all though, because our brains are great at sweeping in vast quantities of information and then sifting it for preferences, likes and dislikes. Small differences can have big impacts. A metal wedge does not have to be large to split open a granite boulder, for example, so *any* difference is a useful difference.

Turn to the Personal Planning Kit and have a look at section 10, which is called, rather dramatically, 'Differentiate or Die' (on page 171). Think about all the things you would like to say, and remind yourself that you are a great, worthwhile, talented person. No matter where you have come from to reach this place, people will buy from you and will often not care a hoot about your history. All they will care about is what you are telling them at the point when you are pitching to them. Then when you have a head full of stuff – any stuff will do for now, as you can always refine it later – write it down.

Once you have had fun with your planning kit, draw up a single-sheet 'flyer' that describes your business and what makes you different. I did this at least 10 times, because each time I went away from it I thought of something new to add and had to update it. Being a catherine wheel I polished it for a week until it shone with a burnished glow.

I showed some samples to my trusted chums and nobody laughed. I even showed a copy to a potential client, who expressed an interest in coaching work, and I nearly fainted. So then, someone actually wanted this stuff? My hunch was right all along: I could strike out on my own and could leave the bastards behind.

When buying promotional literature, take into account all the costs involved in the project and the consequences of doing or not doing it. For example, I once went to order some replacement leaflets in a previous working life, and was told,

'No problem, sir. Two thousand is our minimum order quantity.'

Given that this was about 10 years' supply of glossy literature, I declined to place the order and instead redesigned things so we could cheaply print them out from a PC printer or get a commercial printer to do them digitally. The quality wasn't quite as sharp as more traditional litho printing, but we did save a stack of cash.

It doesn't matter if the unit cost is higher if you use your PC printer, because the flexibility of doing things this way can far outweigh the cost. My own leaflets have been produced like this, and I use high-quality paper to help get round the home-grown feel. Nobody has ever questioned the leaflets or sniffed and said,

'I would have booked you, Richard, but since you have cheapskated your marketing literature, I couldn't possibly contemplate it now.'

Here's a tip: think about how much it will cost to get rid of any marketing literature you pay for. I know a talented copywriter who got a good deal on 5,000 small leaflets and still has 4,950 left six months later. Of course they can be distributed, but this costs money and time to organize. So be cautious; little and often can be the mantra to use when producing your own brochures and flyers.

If you want to go all technological and have electronic leaflets, it's worth investing in a website. Although you aren't required by law to have a website to promote your business, I have found that people seem to derive a sense of comfort if you do have one. There is no rational basis for this, as there are a good few fraudsters on the net, but stacks of people assume that because you have taken the time and effort to put up a page or two, then you must be who you say you are. When I started out, a web-literate designer friend helped me to put together a straightforward site, and I was staggered when people would open a meeting with, 'Been to your site. Pretty good. Liked it.'

Electronic differentiation will probably be the place where it all happens in the near future, as each successive generation becomes more at home with the internet than the last. However, if your target market is about as web-literate as the three blind mice, then your spanking new website could be an instant white elephant. And remember that the old pachyderm is scared of mice.

Finally in our skip down marketing lane, before we indulge in a real-life horror story, we shall take a look at that ever-present tool of business-to-business marketing, the business card. I must admit that my desire for perfection went into overdrive when I produced mine, and I managed to chew through over 30 iterations before settling on the final design, which has never changed. My wife, who is a designer, acted as my marketing department, so you can imagine that between iterations 2 and 29 home life was a little strained. I was in full catherine-wheel mode and eventually burned out, leaving a pretty nasty scorch mark in the study carpet.

Think carefully about doing things with relatives or friends, because you can't bark at them when they make a mess of it, and you may find it difficult to sue them for poor quality and then have to invite them round for Christmas lunch. However, my card made it through the design process and I was very pleased with the litho printed results. My wife was just pleased the whole horrible nightmare was over. She would say, 'Never work for your husband, or at least charge him double' – treble in my case.

For me, the business card is the one thing that really is worth investing in. Good-quality printing is a must because digital printing can still look a little vague in places, and you do tend to use the cards up, so paying the extra is worth it. Also having them professionally designed is sensible, because your skill is likely to be in something else.

Although many people fancy themselves as a business Picasso, in my experience the results can look shoddy and amateurish. My own pitiful efforts bear this out in some style. Good design doesn't have to be flashy or gimmicky, but it can make you look professional and someone to be taken seriously.

However in order to keep things in perspective, a builder colleague had all of his business cards printed onto thick plastic, so that they looked like green credit cards. When I suggested he might like to use card, instead of plastic, he was aghast. He gave me a pitying look and then replied

'How can I grout tiles with a piece of card?'

Please turn to the Personal Planning Kit, to section 11 called 'Marketing Toolbox' (on page 172) and tick the list of items you need to source as part of setting up your business. Remember that there is a cost to each of them.

Who would have thought it? Marketing turns out to be a useful thing to know after all.

As a consumer sucker I am readily seduced by pretty packaging, sexy benefits and those mysterious added-value elements, which I don't know if I will ever use, but seem to crave with every fibre of my wallet. Perhaps that's why I used to grimace at marketing types. They can do a blinding job as long as you're not blinded by their intense and unnerving attachment to exactly the right shade of blue.

Having established the usefulness of some basic marketing, we can indulge ourselves as a reward, by laughing at, and learning from, a company that managed the neat trick of differentiating *and* dying. It was a company that should have known better, but spent too much time listening to the much-gelled big-haired marketing geeks, and not enough time reality-checking its offer with flat-headed and neatly combed accountant types. It's a salutary tale and gives us an opportunity to practise our *schadenfreude* (one of our less well-known national sports) and to remember that if we get too clever for our own boots, someone is likely to steal them when we're not looking.

For those who have not got their copy of *Schadenfreude Monthly* on the coffee table, it's a German word meaning 'that feeling of pleasure or satisfaction that we get when something bad happens to someone else'.

For example, I can remember driving to work one very snowy day and watching with stunned horror as a much winged and alloyed sports-nutter hammered past. I remember thinking, 'Gosh, I hope he knows that the next bend is a sharp left-hander'. Then I remember feeling all warm and cosy inside as I gently rumbled past his now much de-winged and smoking ex-sports car, which was parked unhappily halfway through a hedge at the apex of the bend. Silly idiot.

Such is the guilty pleasure that is *schadenfreude.*

In the summer of 1992 a company blundered in the way that only great corporate hulks can really blunder. Imagine what you would say if a flight to America from Europe cost more than £100, and then I offered you a flight for just £100 and threw in a free vacuum cleaner? 'You're mad!' you would cry. 'That sounds too good to be true!' But alas, for the company in question, Hoover, it was true. Their marketing wizards dreamed up the impossible promotion – impossible, because it just didn't add up. At first they only offered free return flights to Europe, and when their travel agents buckled under the huge demand for tickets they cannily avoided cutting their losses at this point and launched a second promotion to take people to the Good ol' US of A. Not surprisingly this offer was also snapped up. Then, to make matters worse, the press started to sniff about and created tabloid mayhem, once they realized that Hoover's numbers had more flaws in them than a Ming vase that has bounced down the stairs and been hastily glued back together.

Poor old Hoover. Although the press coverage was lavish in its mockery of the promotion, this only served to attract more interest, as people realized that there was, quite literally, a bargain to be had. The word 'fiasco' soon appeared, as demand swamped capacity and the whole saga spiralled out of control. Eventually Hoover had to fight a snowstorm of small claims for compensation, and its proud name was dragged around the departure lounge of life. Although 220,000 people[4] did get to see the inside of a plane, the whole episode became etched on the tombstone of 'Great marketing disasters' and a fair few heads rolled out of the Hoover HQ and onto the job market. After all, the debacle had only cost Hoover around £48 million. Ouch!

For our small businesses, starting to get off the ground, the moral of the story is dead simple. Marketing can be a great way to get yourself known, but you can fuck it up big style if you don't stop and think.

---

4   Source: BBC News website, bbc.co.uk: 'Hoover's free flights fiasco recalled'.

The Big Secret

Tell everyone you know

7

Let's face it, life's a bitch sometimes. Complete with six-inch stilettos, smudged red lipstick and the sort of wild tangled hair that would frighten a mongoose. Dealing with the bitch can mean doing things we dislike, such as paying our taxes or being nice to a big customer who is slow in paying his debts.

A business chum of mine was refused payment by a swine who sold a car on his behalf and then claimed he had no money. Having given him time to pay up, my chum eventually decided to overcome this little hurdle and drove round to his house, armed with a steel-bumpered 4x4. He calmly asked for his cash, but the swine claimed mercy and said he had no money on him.

Nothing, not a nickel.

Suddenly my chum remembered that he had an iron bar in his pocket, which he produced with the same glee as if he had just found a boiled sweet. Just as suddenly, the swine remembered that he had £1,000 in his pocket, which he produced and handed over with a greasy smile. He also decided to pay the balance promptly to avoid seeing his front window being replaced with the backside of the 4x4, which could easily have 'slipped' its handbrake and come screaming through the wall.

Now, clearly I do not condone violence in the pursuit of your business goals, but the story does remind us that, as I said, life's a bitch sometimes and it pays to be resourceful.

Selling yourself is no exception. You put a red light in your window and pose moodily in your leopardskin thong to attract the attention of passers-by in the hope that they will fall for your bulging charms and part with some money. I wonder why leopardskin is considered sexy? I mean, if you were locked in a cage with a leopard I seriously doubt if you would go all wobbly and ask it for a slow dance. Such is the mystery of life.

Certainly, trudging around the country in search of customers I have occasionally felt like a prostitute, except without the advantage of being able to lie down on the job. You get fed up working strange hours of the day and night, meeting the odd git who wastes your time, and having to pander to the demands of people who are not on your Christmas card list. When I started I really didn't appreciate how tiring selling can be when you do it well.

Unless you are only in business as a hobby and simply enjoy the arrogance of hiding behind a façade of respectability, without needing to go through the grind of real work, then selling is going to be top of your list of things to get right. A great business card, super marketing differentiation and a prudent sales forecast are great, but by themselves they are never going to bring money into your business.

However before you leap off your armchair in despair and sprain your wallet, help is at hand, so be still and calm your beating heart. Draw the curtains, blindfold the cat and slide up closer, because the real secret of successful selling is a combination of hard work, persistence, listening and … *networking*.

When I talk to people about networking I am staggered at how many times they just look blank and assume that I have dropped into conversational Cantonese for a moment. If I was to offer you a shady statistic on the subject, it would be that for every member of the networking group I used to belong to, until I needed to fish in a different pond, there were 10 people who visited and said, 'This is just not for me. I don't have the time to network. Too busy running my business.'

Hmm: too busy doing what, exactly? Too busy to go and meet people who might buy their products? Too busy writing reports that no one is going to read, instead of telling people about the great products they sell? Too busy photocopying their fat backside, or trying to grope the receptionist, to go out into the world and actually meet new and interesting people?

Now I have been guilty of saying some of the above, and I would plead for leniency, on the grounds of fear and naivety. The whole thought of networking just seemed, well, a bit grubby to begin with; right up there with baby-kissing politicians, who press the flesh and leave behind the acrid whiff of insincerity. I very nearly didn't do any real networking, claiming that I was far too busy and far too important to do that sort of thing. After all, I was a businessman, not a vote grabber.

How wrong I was. I only changed my mind when my wife reminded me that we needed money to pay for the children's shoes and that this problem would not be cured by sitting at home. So I visited a local networking group (there are loads all over the place) and was staggered at the response.

Firstly, I met all my competitors in one gulp, which was a godsend. If you're good at what you do, then have no fear. I have worked for and with several 'competitors' because we all have slightly different skill sets and backgrounds so will naturally appeal to different people. Meet your competitors and learn from them.

Secondly, I was able to talk about my business in front of 30 people, who listened interestedly, but who really didn't give a shit. This can be quite humbling, and if your head is in the clouds with just how precious and special your business is, then go and talk to a bunch of tired high-street shop owners, builders, plumbers and the like. They will not be impressed with your mighty claims of magical healing powers and will ask dead straight questions, such as:

- Why should I bother to listen to you?
- What can you do for my business now?
- Why should I choose you, when the lady up the road is half your price?

Learn to love these questions and to answer them with the slick honesty of an eel in a top hat and tails. If you can't, then you have a problem.

Thirdly, I met some people who liked what I had to say and were prepared to see me at a follow-up meeting. Follow-up meetings are essential, because they give you a chance to listen to your potential customers and to dovetail your products or services with their needs. Some of these people indirectly helped me to refine my product range, because I went away thinking that although I couldn't help them today, I would make damn sure I would plug the gap and then go back next month. Some of these people just turned into good friends, whom I added to my supporters club. Some of these people wasted my time, and that is the nature of things.

And finally, some of these people booked me.

One booking makes the whole effort worthwhile, and washes away the dirt and grime and doubt of previous failures. Make a sale and you feel like a tycoon, with the world before you. You drive home beaming and being polite to little old ladies in tiny tin cars, who need a periscope to see over the steering wheel and therefore do not enjoy being cut up as you overtake. Save the cutting up for days when you return home with your sales keep-net empty.

Networking is the smart way to travel round your business community, because it takes the heat out of selling. People pass your details on to other people, and someone you have never heard of calls you one day and says that so and so recommended you. This does tend to happen, once your network has been built and maintained, like an ambitious spider roping up a magnificent web to catch bats, having got fed up with an all-fly diet.

Networking is not complicated, and rests on the principle that 'a friend of my friend could be my next customer'. If I know 50 people and I tell them I am looking for a new managing director to coach, then they will all know perhaps 50 people, some of whom may be MDs in need of my tender touch. When they are next together in the pub, or risking a heart attack on the squash court, and the question of support surfaces, then it is possible that my business card will change hands, complete with a 'give this chap a call' sort of intro that money can't buy. Despite my own initial reservations, this kind of result has fallen into my lap.

Because people buy people, a third-party referral is always a more valuable introduction, because people are more relaxed and more prepared to listen to their friend or colleague because they trust them.

The way to successfully network is to make sure you go and talk to people, and ask them *specifically* for what you are looking for. The temptation is there to be vague and just say you would be interested in 'any electrical work going', but unfortunately the human brain prefers to start with specific information and then to generalize subsequently, which means that if you're vague, you're swept up into the general mush of data which we suck up each day. Be specific, and people can easily remember you when the specific need pops up. It's a bit like playing snap, when you only have to remember one thing. Increase your chances of success dramatically, and instead of asking for 'general electrical work', ask for 'garden lighting installation' if that is what you want to do more of.

The acid test of this is your birthday. Next time you are

in line for a cake and a slew of saucy cards, be vague about your present list and I'll bet you'll be disappointed. Ask specifically for what you want, and enjoy receiving a pile of great presents and not having to fake your thank-you smiles.

Always carry business cards with you: in your wallet, in the car, in your kids' lunch boxes, or tucked into the waterproof pocket in your swimming trunks, and hand them out with gleeful abandon. People often keep cards or type them into PDAs, so help them to fill their memory banks with your information. There's no need to feel nervous at this. You are in business because you are good at something. You have a right to network yourself, and if people don't like what you say or how you say it, you're just seeing their stuff and it doesn't diminish you or your talents. Business cards oil the machinery of networking, and without oil, all machines grind to a halt, spewing out sparks on the way.

The first thing to do to get networking is to draw up a big list of who you already know, and to decide what specific thing you will ask them to look out for on your behalf. Turn to section 12 of the Personal Planning Kit, called 'Net-Work' (on page 173) and make a start.

Having thought about networking and constructed a list of people to go and introduce myself to, I have found that there is a great way to get over the fear of actually doing this kind of thing. I hate going up to people and making small talk, preferring instead big silence, which feels safer. One of the concerns that people have when faced with any sort of interview is, what do they say? Which words come out of their mouth? What needs to be said, and what needs to be left behind to keep a few shots in your locker for later? The answer to this is to develop what I call a *skinny minute*, to give yourself some words in order to overcome any networking shyness you may have.

A skinny minute is all about talking for between 30 and 60 seconds and then shutting up and asking a question to get the other person's mouth moving. Talk about you and your products or services and then button it.

Generally it's a good idea to get as close to the magic 60 as possible, because you can say more, but in my experience not everybody is comfortable with this, so choose a length that feels right for you. If you talk for more than a minute, you run a high risk of boring the pants off the person in front of you, and if he's a hairy overweight slob, you will not wish to see him without his hideously baggy undergarments on.

A skinny minute can take practice to hone. I practise mine in the kitchen, to the goldfish and the gerbil, who have proved to be a receptive and uncritical audience. Whenever people ask me how I got to be good at it, I just say practice, and getting it wrong a few times to begin with to remind me of the need to practise.

Before we look in detail at the filling of your steaming hot sales pasty, it's fun to think about some overcooked pies: those magnificent failures, who managed to do more damage to their business in a minute than a whole department of marketing meatheads could manage in a month. In the stocks of business life, ready for us to throw rotten eggs at, come the following people, whom I met at various business meetings, conferences and networking events. Some were unprepared and some were just plain arrogant. A few were overcome by nerves and they are not on the list, as it's OK to be nervous when you start off.

The first person I would like to welcome is the man who forgot his business name, even though it was stitched in neat gold letters on his blue shirt. Then there was the lady who refused to stop talking after her time ran out, and had to be lassoed and dragged from the floor. She didn't go gracefully.

A fair few gentlemen, with more talent that tact, have welcomed the ladies in the room with a bad crack about how nice it is to see some women in business, and then said, trying to generate good humour with a gentle joke, 'Could you get us another coffee, love?' This is a great way to kill to the atmosphere stone dead and turn an audience hostile. Try it if you want to have some fun.

However, the small gold statuette for the singularly most inept performance goes to the man who managed to combine all of the above into one effortless display of ignorance and stupidity, a virtuoso performance truly deserving recognition. The only bit he got right was his name, which was the bit he should have got the most wrong. This would at least have allowed him to sink back into agonizing anonymity.

In a packed room, chock full of local business potential, our hero rose, looked at the group and then said:

'Right, my turn, is it? Um … I haven't prepared anything, so I'll just make it up. As you know my name is Best Boilers and as you know we do – er, what do we do? Er, yes, er, we do boiler stuff and well … you know what we do. And instead of telling you about my business I thought I'd tell you a joke. It's here on my mobile phone. Hang on a sec while I find it.'

He paused and absent-mindedly scratched his groin. Then he fished about in a pocket, pulled out his mobile phone, pushed some buttons and failed to find the joke. Getting desperate he looked around for help, but wisely, none came. Off he went again:

'Oh, for fuck's sake, it was here a minute ago. Stupid fucking phone.'

He turned and threw it hard at the wall, and the whole room watched in stunned silence. The phone bounced onto the floor, gave out a sad little beep and died.

Shrugging off the technical hitch our hero doggedly continued, his credibility badly wounded, but still with enough blood left in him for one final assault.

'Anyway, I'm sure I can remember most of it. There were two hookers, a bishop and a blind man, and the bishop turns to the first hooker and says –'

'Time's up,' sang out the timekeeper. 'Sit down. Next please!'

It was awful to sit through, in the way that a car crash viewed in slow motion has that strange ghoulish fascination to it which keeps you glued to *Police Camera Arseholes* on the telly. Trashing your business reputation and your phone in a minute takes some doing, and is not for the faint hearted. The skinny minute motto here is prepare for success, or prepare for failure. You choose.

Getting a skinny minute sorted out is relatively easy, and just takes a bit of quiet thinking and then a few minutes to jot down your ideas. In my experience there are two ways to talk confidently for about 60 seconds. They are:

- Write 150 words about what you do, what makes you different and what you are looking for. End with a catchy sign off, or a question which throws the ball straight back to the person you are meeting with. You can then read out your notes, if the situation allows.
- Write down eight key points that describe you and

your business and what makes you interesting. These points are the gold nuggets panned out of your marketing blurb or website doodles. You can use them to form the spine of your skinny minute. This is helpful if you need to prepare in a hurry.

When thinking about the structure of your minute, it can help to use these next three areas to give some shape to either your 150-word text, or your list of eight key words. The three areas are:

1. **Introduction.** Thank the person for sparing some time for you. Mention your name and what your business is all about.
2. **Body.** Talk in more detail about no more than three products or services. Avoid the temptation to fill time by listing everything you do. People don't remember lists very easily, so less information has more impact. Do include numbers and quick stories to illustrate your point. We can all remember stories from our childhood, and when you have left the meeting the details will linger on for a while.
3. **Summary.** Revisit any key points if you wish to place a particular emphasis on them, and ask for what you need, if it's useful to do so. Then wrap up with a question or a catchy tag-line, depending on the circumstances.

Using numbers or quick stories is a great way to be remembered. Think about the following examples of how to pin yourself to the notice board of people's subconscious:

I'm a florist with over 100 different types of flowers in stock.

Our training business has helped over 500 people to use a computer.

Last week a man drove all the way from Scotland to have us fix his classic car. That's how good we are.

We sell elephant posing pouches for less than £10.

We specialize in small business accounts and give you free software to help you keep your records in good order.

Did you know that hypnosis can have an 85 per cent success rate in helping people to give up smoking?

Visit Ted's tobacco store. All our cigars are hand-rolled on the thighs of virgins.

To help yourself even more, it can be worthwhile to jot down some key words in the margin of your notepad before you go into a sales meeting. When I dry up, perhaps through nerves, or because I am just tired after a long drive, these prompts are a discreet and helpful way to bring me back on track. Life does not have to be a memory game, and everything you do to help yourself makes your day that little bit easier.

Another tip is to ask for a glass of water. Cups of tea and coffee go cold and bitter, and just when you most want to look happy and smiley you take a sip and grimace. Instead, take a cool sip of water and give yourself a moment to collect your thoughts. It works, and has helped me on several occasions to look like a poised porpoise and not a floundering fish.

So next time you're asked, 'What do you do?', a skinny minute is an effective way of selling your business, without boring the person in front of you. It could look something like this:

> Good morning, Frank, and many thanks for your time today. Paula's Pets is an exotic pet business and we supply a range of reptiles to homes, schools and night club artistes. We've been in business for over five years and have a number of unique products and services.
>
> For example, we have seven different species of poisonous snake currently in stock. We offer schools a great insurance package, in case of bites, and we've trained more than 20 pythons to pole dance. Also, one regular customer was so impressed with our un-kinking service she now advertises us during her act.
>
> This week we're doing a special offer on chameleons, and you may know someone who would be interested. We guarantee that they'll match their wallpaper!
>
> So that's me, Paula's Pets, reptiles for all occasions. Now, I've noticed that Frank's Flies are open and wonder if you'd show me what's inside? (150 words).

A skinny minute delivers useful and relevant information in a precise package. It's easy to listen to, easy to remember and prevents you from waxing lyrical about your own pet business. When I do my own skinny minute I sometimes use my extra-cheesy tag-line to finish with, particularly if I am looking for more coaching work:

> So that's me, Richard Maun. Remember: if you want to get ahead – catch a coach!

I don't mind having fun, or going large on the cheddar slice at the end of the minute. Life doesn't have to be dull.

Pause here and reflect on what your skinny minute could sound like. Then turn to the Personal Planning Kit, to section 13 called, cunningly, 'Your Skinny Minute' (on page 174) and note down the key words that will go into yours. Then take a walk round your garden and practise introducing the flowers to your blossoming business.

Now you have mapped out a skinny minute, there are a smattering of networking tips to smile at. Think about them and then decide which ones will help you to make a success of your business.

Firstly, in time-honoured tradition it helps if you give to receive. Passing business cards and referrals around your own network is a good way to build friendships and establish your reputation as someone to know. Passing business on to other people is rewarding, as we all like to be recommended to a new customer.

Also you don't need to be in selling mode all the time. Some of the best networking meetings I have attended are those where I have just listened to others and collected their cards. Then once back home I have telephoned the ones I'm interested in and offered to go to see them, to learn more about their business. Once in the privacy of their office and without being distracted by a herd of networkers all frantically vying for their attention, I can calmly tell them about me and my business, having listened to them first of course.

Lastly, a network is like a neatly trimmed bush. You need to water it, shuffle out the dead wood and generally keep on top of things. Otherwise you could think you have a great network, when in fact all you have is a bunch of out-of-date business cards. Remember also that all sorts of people network, because it's a cheap and easy way to bring more people to your shop, or past the door of your fledgling business.

We would be wise to doff our caps at the internet once more and be respectful of its possibilities, even if we might be slightly unnerved that the world is being taken over by teenagers, who can now stream live video of themselves miming to some tuneless pop song at any time of the day or night. The world wide wobbly thing can be a useful way of staying in touch with people who are in different parts of the country and even different countries. You start your business in your back bedroom or in your friend's garage and before you know it you're linked across five continents!

So before we dash off to have fun trying to find the stinking fish that can lurk under people's desks, let's recap the *Big Secret* of finding customers.

Networking is the smart way to get around because you get access to more people in a shorter space of time than you would simply by trudging the highways and byways of your local business community.

People really do refer good people to their friends and colleagues, and although it can take a few months to pay off, the effort is rarely wasted. I have collected a bunch of satisfied customers and have used the products and services of people whom I like and trust. This can be helpful when you need your telly fixed, or need to find a great plumber in a hurry.

I have also met my competitors, whom I was a bit wary of at first, but I soon realized that I am just as good as them, which was a real confidence boost. One of my 'competitors' has become a good friend and it's fun to meet up, swap horror stories and chat about the latest developments in our business world.

Networking is often cheaper than business-to-business advertising, it can have a high success rate because of the warm nature of it (as opposed to the chill of cold calling), and it gets you away from the isolation that many people feel when working for themselves, like a champagne cork bobbing about in a menacing grey sea.

It's a fair bet that after a few meetings your confidence will soar and you will become razor-sharp at introducing yourself to others and talking with pride and passion about the great products and services tucked into your portfolio. Smile and wave, hand out your cards and enjoy working your network. And then enjoy spending the money you earn!

Find the Stinking Fish

Clear contracting for success

Driving to an appointment one cold and crisp February I was idly enjoying the thrill of working for myself and being the master of my car and my time when my mobile trilled and I switch on the hands-free earpiece. I suspect that there is a whole generation of sexy young things who will all be deaf in one ear by the time they're 40, from over-use of this useful but penetrating technology. Piping stuff straight into your ear is helpful, but is not what Mother Nature had in mind when she designed the human head.

So there I was, enjoying my day, when technology spoiled it. The call was from Peter, a coaching client who had been hired as an interim manager to work in a scruffy little factory to help the owners improve their production systems. He sounded tired and fed up.

'I'm calling you, Richard, because I've had enough and I want to leave. The bastards are grinding me down and I just can't take it any more.'

'OK, then let's think about it,' I replied, playing for time. 'Don't do anything hasty for now. I'm just about to arrive at a meeting, so my suggestion is that you have a quiet day and we can talk again at lunchtime, or in the evening, and then we can work out the best thing to do.'

'Can't do that,' Peter replied in a faraway voice. 'I've already left. I'm talking to you on the motorway on the way back home.'

Shit! Bugger! I hate days that start with so much sunny promise and then fizzle into drizzle as life steps up and gives you a hard slap in the face.

A month before this conversation took place, I had visited Peter in his factory for the first time and had met the owners, a father and son. The place was a tip and the two people who were supposed to be running it were clearly just floundering in their own inbred uselessness. Family-owned business can be a nightmare to work with, because they operate on emotional lines and give plum jobs to relatives who wouldn't make it as a shit-shoveller in a zoo, such is their general lack of ability. Just because mum or dad gives you a top job doesn't mean that you have any more talent than a cockroach in a business suit. Be nice to your employees, they earn your wages.

During the visit I had asked what they wanted Peter to do. The dad looked at me and explained that he was tired of running the business and wanted to take a back seat, to let his son develop new customers. Therefore, they needed someone to take over the daily management of the business for a bit, while the son went off to do some selling work.

It was January. I looked at the son as dad was telling me this, and noticed that he was neither smiling nor nodding in agreement, so I asked him when his new selling role would begin. 'Um, August, I think,' he said, with a level of conviction that suggested he would only hit the road if his rep mobile was a Ferrari and he was chauffeured by some busty model who could keep her brains next to her handbag in the laughably small glove box. Given the state of the place I would have been surprised if dad had anything more exotic in mind than an old van, driven by the brawny burger-flipping girl from the mobile café across the road.

Although they were both saying they wanted to improve the business, it was clear that dad wanted to do anything except change, and that son was not willing or able to have a go at something new. It's a classic business cop-out. You hire someone else to do the professional job that you have unstintingly failed to do, and then blame them when their progress is slower than you would have liked. You had 20 years to do it, but you give the new guy a whopping two months, while simultaneously unpicking every change he makes, like a man with a pneumatic drill following a road roller.

Dad continued to declaim grandly about the changes he wanted Peter to make, to improve the operational aspects of his little empire, but when Peter suggested a few obvious remedies, like buying a broom, dad sniffed haughtily and said that he would have to authorize all improvements first. It was as obvious as the muck on the floor that dad's business was his baby and it was staying in his own image, which he was comfortable with. Son, who was also his baby, was not about to leave the warmth of his office, and dad had no obvious mettle to chuck him out for going against his wishes. That just left Peter, caught like a thin slice of salami in a fat sandwich, to do the best he could, having now contracted to have a go at the project. If only Peter had known all this before he took the job, then maybe he would have told them politely to sling their offer in the river and could have left them to their drooling misery, while he went and worked for some decent people who meant what they said.

Had Peter developed a nose for a bad smell he might have noticed that under the desks of dad and son were piles of stinking fish, rotting happily in their own oil. Had they been discovered in time they could have been stuffed in plastic bags and disposed of. The office could have been sprayed with a petro-chemical fragrance-enhancing potion and all would have been well. However, now the damage was done and the scent of fish scales was making the atmosphere acrid. Life was going to be tough for Peter, as fishy smells are impossible to remove if you can't deal with the source of the problem.

When you work for yourself, in whatever capacity, the art of clear *contracting* is essential, if you want to manage risk and make sure you get paid on time and to the right amount.

In Peter's case he left this company and soon found

another job. During the interview he asked loads more questions about why the owners wanted change and what they were prepared to do differently in order to improve their business. He listened to them and noticed how much they had budgeted for new equipment and training. He noticed that they nodded and smiled when thinking about the future, instead of grumbling amongst themselves. He had made sure there were no stinking fish under the table. He took the job and was a great success.

People often agree to do a piece of work without taking the time to think about what's going on for the people who have commissioned them. What is it that is swirling round inside their heads that will ultimately determine whether you will be a success or a failure, or whether they are even prepared to give you a chance to show your worth?

Customers can be funny creatures, and often don't tell you what they really want, the first time you ask them. It can take them several attempts to be specific. The art of clear contracting is about drilling down through the heavy clay in their minds to reach the bedrock of truth which sits several metres down.

When a customer says she wants the walls painted white, does she really mean apple-white or peach-white? When a man asks for a haircut, does he mean a quick trim or a full-scale restyle? When a woman asks for a bunch of flowers for 'about £20', does she mean less than £20, or more than £20? Clear contracting is about making sure all the details are brought out into the open so that the people supplying the goods or services can make informed and practical business decisions.

When working for yourself it is too easy to be carried away by the success of making a sale to bother stopping and pondering on the whole situation. I was wrong-footed once when a call came through to book me for some training work. The manager asked for a price and I happily quoted a daily fee rate, inclusive of all materials. 'Oh great,' he said. 'That's great value, thank you.'

This was alarming news. I don't mind being reasonably priced, but 'great value' smacks of a cheap giveaway. Based on a previous conversation I had assumed that there would be just six people to be trained and had priced accordingly. However, the 'great value' had triggered an alarm bell, which clonked dully in my head. I weakly asked how many delegates there would be.

'Sixteen,' came the bright reply.

What? Sixteen! That would mean more handouts to print and more planning time to make sure the day would run smoothly. It would mean making sure I took more resources on the day, and it would mean I would have to work harder for my fee! However, it can look a bit sick if you go back to your client and say, 'Sorry, I made a mistake when I gave you that price. What I meant to say was the cost would be ....'

You can try to repair the damage, but a good rule in contracting is that it's one hundred times easier to *reduce* a price after reflection than it is to raise it. When you raise a price, people feel put upon and can feel that you are taking their goodwill for a fast ride on a corkscrewing roller-coaster. They might agree to the sudden price hike and still book you, but they will also tend to sulk and might never book you again. In this case, for me the damage was done. I could hardly cough, say I had made a mistake, and then suddenly double my fee.

Fortunately the job went well and the client was happy. I wrote off my smaller fee to experience and 'goodwill', and for subsequent work asked for a higher price. The clients didn't mind because they had liked working with me and felt confident that I was worth the extra money.

However, I did get an extra kick in my soft parts while running the course. During the lunch break I happened to look at the menu, and realized that per head my fee was cheaper than a buffet for 16, with coffee and sticky buns. Sometimes it's a bit crushing to find out that you're worth less than a sponge finger.

Enthusiasm for what you do is great, but don't let it get in the way of a pragmatic and hard-headed business deal. Ever since that experience I have used a three-stage strategy to help get the price right when contracting:

1. Always find out the details before you quote. Think about size, timescale to completion, complexity, materials to be purchased and the time taken for the invoice to be paid.
2. Value yourself and your expertise. Ask for a fee or set a price that you feel justifies the product or service on offer. Remember to mention your differentiating factors in support, if you feel you need to.
3. If you have to quote on the spot, then offer a higher price, to cover yourself against lack of information. You can always reduce it when you have had more discussions.

Clear contracting is all about finding out the details of the work to be done, so that there are no hidden fish to go smelly and spoil the project. It sounds obvious, but most people I have met have a horror story or two about the time when it all went horribly wrong for them.

There are three parts to clean contracting, two which are commonly known and one which is not.

The first part is the basic *administrative details* that we all take for granted. Most people will take a booking for their services and put the date into the diary. Admin details include dates, times, length of appointment, fees, handouts, reports to be written or photos to snap. Location helps too, as does the 'who does what' bit. I generally get the client to do as much work as possible: not through my own laziness, but simply out of expediency. If you are the one who books the room and the food and organizes the whole thing, then a simple day's work can turn into a multi-headed monster before you know it, as each interested party calls you up with his or her preferences and pet dislikes – unless of course you are a party planner, in which case this kind of aggravation is where you get your kicks. No, I prefer to concentrate on what I do well and leave the mundane (but dangerous if you get them wrong) details to someone else.

If you are a landscape gardener, then it can help to use a day-book to write in all the details when clients phone you to place an order. If they change their mind you could be the one facing the cost of throwing away the wrong type of turf, so take time to take down the details and protect yourself. The same goes for builders, electricians and the like. It can be dangerous if you take a call in your van and simply remind yourself to write down the details later. Better to pull over and make some notes there and then, as people's memories can be notoriously unreliable.

The second area of contracting looks at the *goals* the customer wants you to achieve and the process you will use to get there. Great goals are precise and achievable. A client turning up at a hairdresser wanting to be transformed into a skinny pop princess may be too ambitious. A retired couple who invite a builder to 'Just build us a conservatory' are likely to be disappointed when the finished article doesn't look like their imagination.

If clients ask for something that you feel is beyond your capability, it's important to tell them and not get yourself sucked into a contract that you can't complete. If you start something you can't finish, you may get sued.

The process may be different depending on your occupation. For me as a management trainer there are different ways of facilitating a group. For a builder, the process of building an extension may require someone's prize flower bed to be dug up, or the fitting of a new kitchen may create more dust than a Saharan sandstorm. Agreeing what will happen between starting and finishing the job is a good way to keep clients on your side.

Finally we swim down to the fishy level, where, not surprisingly, the fish live. They often don't smell to begin with, but if you don't deal with them they have a nasty habit of hanging around. Once out of water they die and then rot gently as a way of attracting your attention to them. The trouble is, people don't like the smell, so they may ignore them in the hope that they will just fade away. They don't. They hang around until they have been dealt with.

This is what happened in Peter's story. The dad and son could have told him they were scared of change, but that in itself would have been a scary thing to admit. Much better to keep it secret and hope that some new person, or event, will push them through the pain barrier. The trouble is that the fish get in the way. They are our fears and concerns, and until we talk about them they just swim around until they die.

When contracting for success some useful questions to ask, in order to find the fish before they can do any smelly damage, are:

- What don't you like?
- What concerns do you have?
- What 'dumb' questions would you like to ask?
- Are there any secret things you need to mention?

- What has not worked well for you in the past?
- What happens if we don't finish the contract on time?
- What does the word 'change' mean to you?
- What will you say if your new hairstyle doesn't suit your face shape?

Each question invites the customer to think about their emotional response to the situation. Dumb questions are great questions, so giving people permission to ask them can be a really smart way of helping them unlock their fears or their worries.

Often people are not able to say exactly what they would like, but they can tell you precisely what they don't like. Finding out these negatives helps you to bump into the boundaries bordering your freedom to work.

So the third part of clean contracting is all about the stuff which we have in our heads, which we may or may not share with people when the agreement to do the work is being forged. These things are the *fish* which we need to go trawling for, before they sabotage the whole operation.

Stop at this point and think again about the story of Peter, the dad and his son. Ask yourself what three questions he could have asked during his interview to find out where the stinking fish were. Then turn to the Personal Planning Kit, to section 14 called simply 'Trawling' (on page 175) and write them down.

Peter's story also illustrates the importance of understanding *all* the people involved in the contract. Although it looked like dad made all the running, the son was an important player too, and was someone to think about when gaining agreement over how and what work would be done.

It can help to draw a map of the people involved and connect them to each other, to illustrate who has agreements with whom. A colleague of mine had a tricky situation and when we discussed it she was not sure what to do resolve a problem she had with the managing director. When we mapped all the parties she realized that the company chairman was the father of the MD, someone who clearly exerted an influence, but she had never spoken with him as he only rarely visited the business. Once we mapped it, it was obvious that to resolve the organizational deadlock she needed to speak with the chairman and understand his needs and expectations, as they were influencing the MD, his son, and hence the whole project.

When meeting with a client, particularly for consultancy work, or training, it can be really helpful to list all the management people with a vested interest in that project, and then to plot them on a piece of paper to ensure you have a clear agreement with each one. The same applies if you're organizing a wedding, or planning a party.

An example of a contract map is shown overleaf, for a piece of training work. If you are the trainer then you may need to contact each person you are connected to, in order to make sure that the expectations for the day are clearly understood and agreed between you. Although it is unlikely that you will talk to all the delegates before the day, it is probable that you will send them some joining instructions, so that they know where to go and what to expect. Also, a smart trainer will start the day with an agreement between himself (or herself) and the delegates, to ensure they all know what the day will look like, when breaks will be, if it's OK to ask questions and to clarify points as needed.

A contract map for training services

All of this work sets the scene for a successful day, which will result in you being paid and hopefully asked back.

If you're not convinced about stinking fish and contract maps, then do some work with sloppy contracts, or perhaps engage your friendly builder to whack up an extension and instead of a clear agreement just wave vaguely at the side of your house say, 'Plonk it over there, mate. I'm sure that will do fine. I'll leave it you, then.' If all this sounds a bit extravagant, for some sorts of business it can be. However, all people providing services contract with their clients, and all clients have views, opinions, concerns and questions. Once you have understood them, you can contract cleanly for success. There will be no stinking fish waiting to cause a nuisance or even stop the project, which could be a disaster for you if you have already committed time and effort and purchased materials.

Stinking fish are everywhere, lurking in the depths of office cupboards, under desks and in briefcases and handbags. Given that your continued business success is important to you, you can ask questions and you can check things out. If you do, you will probably sleep better and deliver an even more impressively high-quality service to your delighted customers. If you don't then what happened to me could happen to you.

I once drove 200 miles to an appointment and turned up fully armed and ready for work. 'Hello Richard,' cooed the receptionist. 'And what are you doing here today?'

That was not the greeting I had expected. 'I had an email last month to book the appointment ...' I began.

'Oh, did you? Well that was just to ask if you *could* join us. Did you not *check* that we *did* need you? Which we *don't.*'

'Apparently not,' I answered politely, and left with as much dignity as one can muster in these kind of situations, namely sod all. Filing the experience away in my head under 'piss-poor contracting', I then had another 200 miles to while away. By the time I arrived home, I was very fed up and determined not to repeat the exercise.

Before we move on to the next exciting slice of repertoire that is helpful to have when we leave the bastards behind, here is a fishy poem, to summarize the need for clear contracting:

Find the Stinking Fish
Beware beware,
The fish are lurking all around.
Waiting to die,
Waiting to be found.
Because if they stay
Hidden away,
They will stink
And you will say:
'Oh how I wish,
I had trawled for fish,
Before this terribly smelly day!'

Think about it. Clients love clear contracting. They tend to trust people who make detailed transparent agreements, and then who deliver their expectations on time and to the agreed level of quality.

Leaving the fish in our wake to join the networking skinny minute and our differentiating factors, it's time to return to the port of people and think again a bit more about ourselves. This time, though, we are not interested in skills and talents, but instead we are interested in enthusiasm, fear and the mix between the two, which will help to determine whether we have what it takes to stay in the game long enough to become successful.

Unlike the Fireworks Code which looked at the sort of style we tend to exhibit when working under pressure, now we shall think about the different phases we go through when we set up shop on our own. In other words, we shall think about the nature of *transition*.

How Short Are You?

Understanding transition

9

Even more important to your business than the sticky logo on the side of your van, or the super-slick website, or the latest pair of must-have snippy scissors, is the person who makes it all happen. No, that's not your bank manager, or your mate who pushes the odd beer at you to keep you sane. We are again talking about *you*, and your journey from a cute, vulnerable little acorn to a gnarled and majestic oak tree.

We are great people, and we have talent and friends and even rakish good looks. On the flipside we also have a few flaws that we know about. We might be a bit vain or a bit shy, or we might be great with numbers, but poor with written work. There is no need to be magnificently talented in all things businessy, because that would be a ridiculous aim and far too high a target for us to reach. Instead it's fine to be just good enough. That will see us through most things, and if we need particular skills, such as finance, then we can buy them in when required.

One skill to have and to hone is to be aware of the stage that we are currently in on our journey from fed-up wage slave to enthusiastic selfer. People often don't talk about the pain and fear of being your own boss. They munch their *petits fours*, boast about their success and never once mention the tough times that they rode through to get to this particular party.

Take Daedalus for example, one of the very first selfers, who set up his own inventing business several thousand years ago in Ancient Greece, when the internet was just a twinkle in the Gods' eyes and reality television was not even a sketch on Galileo's laptop. Daedalus was a bright spark, and had he lived today he would have been a computing genius of substantial fortune, complete with thick glasses and an inability to talk to girls.

One of his first projects was to construct a wooden cow

for the Queen of Athens, a sparky young woman called Pasiphae. At the meeting to commission the project, Daedalus was careful to understand the nature of the contract he was being offered.

'So then, ma'am, let me see if I have listened closely enough. You want me to make a life-size wooden cow, so that you can hide in it and get royally pleasured by that enormous steaming bull which Poseidon sent you as a late birthday present?'

'That's right, Daedalus.'

'That enormous white bull, with the enormous ...'

'Yes, Daedalus. I wish to show my appreciation.'

'Hmm ... I see, ma'am. Wouldn't it just be easier to post him a thank-you letter?'

The cow was built, and before Pasiphae could say 'bovine' she was pregnant with what would eventually become the Minotaur, the mad half-man half-bull creature who was a bugger to look after when he was in nappies. Daedalus even constructed a labyrinth for him, to keep him out of mischief, after he had butted a succession of well-meaning, but ultimately useless nannies. Then the great Daedalus, inventor and builder of cows, came unstuck when Pasiphae asked him to assist the hero Theseus to escape the labyrinth, after he had bravely slaughtered her dangerous mutant offspring.

Daedalus, who was never one to resist a challenge, thought about it and duly obliged by handing Theseus a long strong thread, which he could use to retrace his steps back to the beginning. The ball-of-string approach worked and Theseus lopped off the Minotaur's head, before successfully navigating his way back to the entrance and the gift shop.

Unfortunately for Daedalus, Theseus helped himself to

the King's daughter on the way out, instead of a cuddly Minotaur key-ring. On hearing of the drama, Minos, the King, flew into a terrible rage and called for revenge. He was too late to catch Theseus, but seeing the ball of string by the entrance he realized that only one man could have invented such a fiendishly clever machine, and locked Daedalus and his son in the labyrinth. They were left to die, with neither hope nor string.

After this turn of events most people would have realized their inventing business was getting out of hand, but not Daedy. He immediately invented a set of feathery wings and escaped the labyrinth by flying away. The only problem was that his son, Icarus, flew too close to the sun, the wax holding the plumage on his wings melted and he plunged to his death, leaving a distraught Daedalus to complete a bulky health and safety report and to fund a massive jump in his professional indemnity insurance premium.

And the point of this particular Greek tragedy is this: working for yourself is an adventure. Like all adventures it has a start and a middle and at some point an end. Where you are in your adventure is up to you, but all adventures have one thing in common. They come in stages, and each stage has its own distinctive feel.

Transition influences our behaviour and lurks in the background watching over us. We all transition through life, from gurgling baby through to wobbly geriatric, and being in business is no different. When we first venture forth on our own we go back to the beginning and start over from scratch. We have to transit from cosy employment to frosty self-employment, and then we have to transit through the foundation and growth of our business.

You might be a legal eagle with a beaky nose and fancy feathers, or a gardener with the world's biggest dibber, but when you walk away from the cosy confines of employment and start off as a one-man band, then no matter who you *were*, you ping straight back to the *beginning*. You have no idea whether you have the capability or stamina to make a fair fist of it, but you will be brimming with bravado and will relish telling your ex-boss that he can go and shove his appraisal up his backside and park it next to his brain.

All people go through periods of transition in their lives, whether it is from married without kids and a life, to married with kids and no life. Our hair goes from soft and fuzzy, through pubescent spikes and colours, to middle-aged greying respectability and finally to soft and fuzzy again. The same is true of people working for themselves, and knowing which period of transition we are in can save us from a fate worse than Daedalus.

It's also helpful to realize that it's perfectly *normal* to have fluctuations in our emotions, and that on some days we will stare out into the grey cold rain and wonder why we are doing this. On other days we will cartwheel up the garden path, shedding our clothes as we go and spend the rest of the day making mad passionate love to our partner. After all, everyone needs a cherry on their cake sometimes.

There are five basic stages of transition which people work through between leaving their old job and becoming happy and secure working for themselves. The fifth stage can be as dangerous as the first three, and the trick is to stay in stage four. For fun we will call our transitional model (see overleaf) **The Height Chart**, and you can see where you fit in. The age is the age of your business, if you were wondering whether you need a squirt of growth hormone to power you through the stages.

You can be in different stages in different situations. For example, you can be a baby when it comes to finance and at the same time be a teenager when it comes to sales. If

The Height Chart

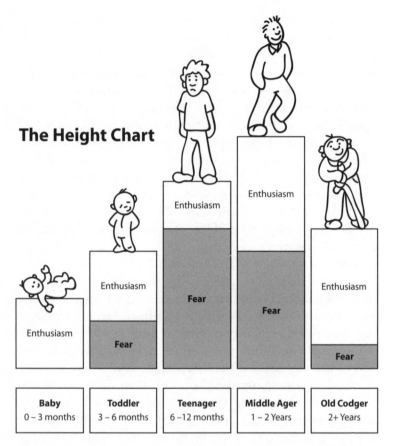

Baby	Toddler	Teenager	Middle Ager	Old Codger
0 – 3 months	3 – 6 months	6 –12 months	1 – 2 Years	2+ Years

you take a knock you may slip back a stage, or if you reflect on your experience you might go forwards, perhaps into middle age. Working through each stage is part of the adventure that we all take when we decide to leave the bastards behind. The following descriptions will help you to decide where you are.

Babies are born full of energy and hope, which can be the way that we all start out. This stage may only last a moment, but that flash of future promise will sow the seed that germinates into a sunflower of an idea, poking out of the top of our heads. Babies don't tend to experience fear, as their world is full of smiling people, who either play with them or stick a big wet nipple in their mouth. Life doesn't get any better really.

Clearly being a baby has its fun element. However, staying a baby is not going to help us launch our business, so we need to put the nipples away and get on with making our legs earn their keep. We need to start walking.

In practice this means going out and talking to people, researching the market and assembling our financial information. This is the **toddler** stage. Many people seem to stay in the toddler stage for several months, until they stumble into success or the money runs out or they bump into a regular job and give it all up. Toddlers tend to get nervous and hold on to the sides of tables and chairs to stop themselves falling over. We can do the same with our business, but at some time we have to let go and get on with the gritty stuff, which for most people is selling.

Once we have learned to walk a bit we find that life isn't too bad and we start to enjoy it. Business picks up and our forecasts might even be not such bad guesses after all. Flowers bloom and little songbirds cheep happily on the windowsill of our happiness.

Then it all changes, dark clouds blot out the sun and the birds fly away to hide. We have met the **teenage** stage, when life is suddenly full of pubescent angst and uncertainty.

Nobody understands us and we hang around street corners trying to look moodily cool, dressed in odd clothes with our hair sprayed with sticky sugar-water and back-combed into the shape of a chicken. We demand to paint our office black, to match our mood and we become an overnight expert in that teenage speciality of sulking.

Lots of people get to a point in the start-up period of their business, usually after their first couple of sales knocks, when they wonder what it's all about. Their confidence takes a tumble and they look gloomily at the flash kit they have purchased and wonder if it will ever be used. Will it end up as an expensive white elephant, they ask themselves?

Some people give up at this point.

It's OK to experience doubts and to take a two-minute holiday to remind yourself why you started on the journey. The teenage period will pass if you keep going, and although you may enter **middle age** with chest hair and cellulite, the arrival will be worth the effort.

At the middle-age stage people will have had the rough edges of their skills polished smooth, and will be in that place where enthusiasm and success are balanced with the fear of losing it. Fear is good. It keeps us in check and stops us sliding into complacency, like a wildebeest on a helter-skelter run by a group of hungry fairground crocodiles.

Stay balanced and business could be good. A bit of fear will prod us into making sales trips to keep exploring new opportunities. Fear will help us to be cautious about future budgets, and will nudge us into continuously developing our products and services. Middle age is the place to be, and you can stay in the middle-age stage for as long as you like.

However, if you spend more than six months without meeting a potential new customer, or refining your products, or smartening up your skinny minute, or dusting the stock in your shop, then you have moved past middle age and have slipped quietly and uncomplainingly into the **old codger** stage.

This is the flipside of the teenage stage, where you glide serenely through your day and marvel at how clever you've been. You may even tut-tut sympathetically when hearing of the demise of a contemporary, and mutter that if only they'd been as clever as you they might still be in business.

Watch out. If you're in the land of slippers, cardigans and buttery toffees, then you're just a slow walk away from a wee-bag and a winding-up order. Plenty of people have gone *phut* and faded away during an afternoon tea break, when the world is engrossed in dunking digestive biscuits.

Not all businesses grow every month or every year. Some periods may be slow, and at times you may even wonder whether you are going backwards. However, if you have continued to meet potential customers, there is always hope out there. You can paddle out of the way of the crocodiles and can make it back into the paradoxical safety of the middle-age stage. The paradox is that more fear means more motivation, although too much fear can paralyse you into inaction. Too little can seduce you into cosy afternoon chat shows on the television and the hidden dangers of lacing Battenberg cake with dry sherry.

Think about where you are now on the height chart, and check your guess with the last person you kissed today. Remind yourself what it means to be in this particular stage, and if you disagree with your stage-checker, go with them and ignore your own guess. Then put a note into your diary and recheck where you are in a fortnight.

On the model each stage has a suggested timescale attached to it as a rough guide. Some people may linger in a stage, others may lollop through it. Some selfers can stay middle-aged for many years and continue to grow their business, others may get a blue rinse and a face lift the day after the day after their first sale.

Before turning to your personal planning kit, read the

following descriptions and ask yourself whether you have said anything similar. What we say out loud is a good indication of what's milling around in the dusty depths of our brain, unless you happen to be in marketing, in which case your little brain will be sitting on the next bar stool, in a gold lamé suit, sipping a martini. He's happy there. Leave him alone with his olive. For the rest of us, read and think.

Baby. I have just been born and everything is full of promise and hope. I am cute and lovable and people will give me a chance to be myself for a change, and will love me for my skills and not for being 'the manager'. I have some talent that I wish to sell to people, and I need to learn some new skills quick. The world is full of sun. Going to work seems like a treat and not a chore. I say to myself, 'Why didn't I do this before?' and 'Wow, nice nipples!'

Toddler. I am so clever because I have been in business for a while and have started to make contacts and spend some money. It's all very exciting and I just love going to 'work' each day. I've met some interesting people and I'm sure they will all buy from me. I still need a guiding hand and I am grateful for the support. The world is sunny and breezy, and I say to myself: 'Why did I listen to those who said it would be tough? I found it easy. Maybe they're just not as good as me.'

Teenager. I'm so fed up. Everyone hates me and I hate them. Especially those people who keep telling me what to do. What do they know about anything? I'm in a mess and I feel like painting my office black and going for a sulk. I have spent more than I budgeted for and nobody seems to understand what I am offering them. I hate them all. Working for yourself seems so thankless and it's taken over my life. All my forecasts are wrong and I drag myself off to networking meetings, which are getting on my nerves. And I've got spots. The world is full of fog and sleet and I wish I'd listened to those people who said, 'Don't do it, you'll soon get a proper job.'

Middle Ager. I am tired and happy. I have good days and I have down days, but on all days I smile and remind myself that I have successfully left the bastards behind. I have continued to slog round my network and it has finally started to pay off. My income is supporting the household budget and my business is sustainable. My forecasts have been revised and I'm now much more cautious when it comes to spending money. The world is full of sun, with a few grey clouds scudding about. If it looks like rain I carry my umbrella. I tell others that 'You can do it too, if you really want to.'

Old Codger. I am warm and comfortable. My slippers are snug. There is great television on after lunch and then I have a corporate snooze. I have had all my clients for the last five years and stopped learning new things a long time ago. My income has fallen, but I don't need to do any networking as my reputation alone is enough to bring people to me. The sun is setting gently in the west and I don't see the hungry wolves approaching from the east. I lecture others and ask, 'Why do you need to keep investing money in new things?'

The place to be on the Height Chart is middle age, and most people only get there once they have worked through the preceding stages. If you're tempted to try and skip the baby, toddler and teenager stages, be careful. These stages bring with it the experience that helps to keep you in middle age, and that stops you snoozing your way incautiously into old codgerdom.

Stop here and think about which category you fall into. Most people start with Baby, but if you are already in business you may have moved on. Turn to the Personal Planning Kit, to section 15 called 'The Height Chart' (on page 176) and note down where you are. Then ask your partner or friend to double-check it for you. The chances are that you will have over-estimated and it won't hurt to dip into reality.

Feelings also keep you in middle age. The elation of success tempered by the fear of losing it all if you don't keep on developing and refining, monitoring and checking. It's OK to have feelings and it's OK to get pissed off sometimes.

If you're a dry old oak tree and immune to feelings, then watch out when the next hurricane hits, because it can push you over in a blink and 200 years of gentle growth can come crashing down in an instant. Majesty becomes matchsticks.

Going through a process of transition is generally tough. It can seem easy to look at the Height Chart and laugh at the moves from baby through toddler and teenager to middle age, but the reality can be harsh. People often don't know where they are today, they only know where they were yesterday, with the benefit of hindsight, so check in with your supporters club from time to time. Ask them where they think you are, and don't take offence when they tell you that they are sitting in front of a grumpy teenager, or a wide-eyed baby with more hope than common sense.

When I started out I was definitely a baby, gurgling and cooing at every new twist of setting up my business.

Choosing a name, designing business cards and messing with a logo were exciting and refreshing. For once I was sitting in my own chair, doing what I wanted to do, with no real appreciation of the toil that stretched out in front of me.

When you go from a salary to nothing there are still bills to be paid, and there are still people around you who worry on your behalf. In my head I knew I was doing the right thing, but to some of those watching me I was caught in the passion of my project and closed to their worries and their concerns. I had a nipple stuck in my mouth and I didn't appear to be letting go.

Transition is necessary in order to be successful, and it is inescapable. Knowing where you are on the height chart is a useful litmus test of your current state of mind. We all have a mix of fear and enthusiasm, and making sure they are in tension is a good way to stay safe and sane during the hard slog of self-employment. Too much fear and we do nothing, or make hasty decisions. Too much enthusiasm and we do too much, but still make hasty decisions.

Celebrate being you, and laugh at yourself when you find you are currently sulking like a grumpy teenager, or slumped in your armchair watching *Celebrity Orgasm* on television, when you should be plodding through your accounts.

I had to take the nipple out of my mouth and get on with it. Now I'm a happy middle ager, although I have slipped and skidded through all the stages on the way to getting there, and have the scars to prove it. Business is an adventure, and it pays to know whether you are a tiny little acorn or a mighty sprawling oak. Staying in middle age is about staying supple, and that requires a mix of emotions. It's OK to have emotions and it's OK to acknowledge them. It's all part of the mix that we encounter when we leave the bastards behind.

Another part of the mix is the cash we have in our business, because that powers our future and keeps us safe in the present. However before we talk about that, we shall pause for a moment to recharge our batteries and have some fun with a spot of playtime.

Yippee, let's go and splash in puddles, or sneak off behind the bike sheds for a crafty fag!

Playtime Kiddo

Stop and smell the flowers

Stop for a second and remember you have a life.

Ha, just kidding!

You have no life, you are working for yourself.

Think about your inner 'kid' for a moment and let him, or her, run about and smell the daisies. Spend a couple of minutes on a favourite hobby, or run to the end of the garden and back.

Was that nice?

Good.

Break time's over and it's back to work.

It's time to meet the bit we have put off until last, the bit that everyone enjoys the most. Yes, ladies and gentlemen it's time to think about some financial aspects of running your baby business. But as I am not an accountant I am not going to bore the trousers off you with dull numberspeak. Instead we are going to begin with a story.

It's a story with a sting in the tail.

The Sunny Afternoon

Practical accounting stories

Business finance is, like Christmas shopping, one of the necessary evils in life. You don't want to do it, you put it off to the last minute, but you know that if you don't attack it you will end up embarrassed in the end.

However, the good news is that finance doesn't have to be dull. We have already talked a bit about pricing, forecasts and the need to understand our costs. We have also established that accountants are great sources of information, and they keep up with the law, which can be updated with more regularity than a politician's mistress. The short cut to easy financial management is to get a good accountant and make him earn his fee.

Don't be resentful that it costs you money for his services. Instead, think of it as an investment in your business, which will reduce the risk of a financial fuck-up and will keep you away from the snapping jaws of the tax man or the VAT man. These people are tough, thorough and professional, and unlike certain breeds of dangerous dog they are not required to be muzzled in public. Keep your affairs in order, or keep an eye out for a nasty letter from one of her Majesty's numerically knowledgeable servants.

To illustrate this point and to draw your attention to the difference between cash and profit, which is a common confusion in my experience, listen to the following story and ask yourself how you would have managed your financial affairs if you had been in the same situation.

It was a warm afternoon in a rather smart hotel, next to a smart golf course, festooned with people in wacky jumpers, all driving smart electric buggies. The back of the hotel had a rather pleasant lounge, where you could sit and enjoy the sun and do a bit of networking, or in my case, coaching.

On this particular afternoon I was meeting with a client, a plumber by the name of Steve, whom I liked but was worried about. Last time we had met we had talked about the need for him to work out a cashflow forecast and to compile a basic profit and loss account to keep track of his finances. He had been trading for over two years and had yet to get to grips with these essential sources of information. We had worked through some ways of producing basic financial summaries, and he had agreed the importance of the need to know where his cash was tied up and what it was doing in his business.

Indeed, I would say that if you don't produce a cashflow forecast then you would be safer to stand naked on the middle lane of any motorway and wave your tackle at passing trucks. Ho ho, you laugh, but that would be insane. And that's my point. In business terms that's what you're doing if you don't know whether your cash is flowing in or is ebbing out, today, tomorrow, and more importantly in six months' time.

As I was talking with Steve, I noticed that a group of mature lady golfers were slowly taking over the lounge, like some green creeper that engulfs your house and blots out the light through the windows. After 20 minutes of chair shuffling, the ladies had cut us off from the exit and the toilets and had proceeded to hold their annual post-match luncheon and award ceremony. Prizes were handed out for the best putt, the longest drive and the person with the brightest blue rinse. Against this surreal business backdrop, Steve produced his laptop, powered it up and proceeded to dazzle me with a sparkling new accounts package which he had spent a week pumping data into.

Now, I was born a bit of a Luddite[5] and have a healthy

---

5 The Luddite movement began in 1811 and was named after its mythical leader, Ned Ludd. The people in the movement were skilled stocking knitters who opposed the introduction of modern weaving technology because of the hardship and the social changes

scepticism for all things electronic, and in particular, people's need to cling to computer software to do their thinking for them. Some programmes are undoubtedly useful, but in the context of successfully running your own business it can be dangerous to be seduced by glitz and glamour and not really appreciate what it is you are being told. Accounting is a great example of this. Using a software package can save time and can look great, but the process of calculation is hidden from your sight. For the uninformed, this deprives you of the understanding you gain by working things out longhand on a piece of paper.

Sitting next to Steve, I watched with saucer-wide eyes as he deftly pushed buttons, clicked options and waltzed his mouse around a ballroom-sized set of numbers. 'Look at this,' he said, smiling. 'I can produce all sorts of graphs and charts to show what's happening in my business.'

Pow! Zap! Kerzang! The charts exploded onto the screen in a shower of light and colour. Wow! I though. Perhaps I *have* got it wrong. Perhaps I should let go of my prejudices and invest in some of this wizardry. Then I asked him to pull up his profit and loss account and show me some real numbers.

'Of course,' he replied. 'Easy.' Click, ping! And there it was.

I looked at the numbers and my heart sank. Not only did he not understand the numbers, but even worse for me, he couldn't even afford my services. Opposite is what I saw.

---

it brought. They protested, smashed up some machinery and were hanged. This made them even more cross. Today the term is often used to describe someone who is against technology. In this case I am using the word to describe my reluctance to be swept along by the rise and rise of labour-saving computer programs, because they can fog us from understanding how things really work. Bring back the chalk and slate!

Steve the Plumber
Profit & Loss Account

	2002		2001	
	£	£	£	£
Sales	40,000		30,000	
Cost of materials	20,000		15,000	
Cost of labour	6,000		0	
Gross Profit		14,000		15,000
Overheads				
Office rent	2,000		2,000	
Heat & light	1,000		1,000	
Van hire	3,000		1,500	
Diesel	2,000		1,000	
Stationery	500		500	
Advertising	2,000		1,000	
Mobile phone	500		500	
Accountancy	1,000		1,000	
Bad debt	2,000		0	
Total Overhead		14,000		8,500
Net Profit		0		6,500

The numbers are similar in scale to what he showed me, but have been simplified to make the P&L quicker to read. The bottom-line difference between the years is as it was on that sunny afternoon, with a wall of happy, chatting lady golfers providing the backdrop to some seriously profound business lessons. To help make sense of the numbers, below are some explanatory notes to assist your thinking about what happened between 2001 and 2002. They also have been simplified and should not be taken as literal truths for your own budgeting purposes!

- Vans cost £1,500 per year to hire.
- Diesel costs are always two-thirds of the cost of van hire.
- Extra workers cost £3,000 each to hire.
- An office can be rented for as little as £500 per year.
- Heat and light costs are always half the rent of the office.
- An accountant can cost only £500.
- Bad debts occur when someone doesn't pay. Steve is also unsure whether Mrs Jones will pay him £1,000 this year (2003).

Profit and loss is all about making sure your overheads don't eat away your gross profit, so that you do actually get left with some *net* profit at the end of the day. However you can't spend profit, because it only shows the cumulative effective of costs and sales in your business over a period of time. Whether you have any *cash* in the bank is another thing entirely, which we shall come to when we tell our next story.

The way to best understand any accounting spreadsheet is to simply ask yourself:

'What's going on? What's the story?'

If we look at the two trading years shown above, there is a clear story, but what is it? Here is the best way to really dig around and find out what is happening.

Firstly, take a pencil and circle all the items that have changed significantly between the years.

What do you notice?

What leaps out at you?

Secondly, give the story a title, such as 'The year I did no selling' or 'How I screwed up my business'. Titles are good, they set they scene for the detail that is to follow. What title would you give this story? Go back a page and scribble something in the margins. Remember that although the example has been disguised to protect the ignorant, the story is a true one. Including the golfers.

Note here that bad debt was a cost to Steve's business. This is because he had already invoiced for the sale and had spent money on labour and materials. Not being paid needs to be reflected on the spreadsheet, otherwise his profit would have been artificially inflated.

My title for this sad little story would be, 'Steve expanded too quickly and turned himself into a manager and stopped working on the tools, when his business could not afford for him to do so'. Another title might be 'Steve increased the costs of his business without increasing his sales sufficiently to cover these costs'.

For a moment Steve and I gazed at the numbers, and then I broke the silence. 'Do you understand what this is telling you?' I asked, reasonably.

'No,' he replied flatly. 'I was hoping you would help me.'

So I explained that the big fat *zero* meant neither profit nor loss, which was a problem if he still intended to take some wages out of his business.

'That makes sense now,' he said. 'I wondered why I didn't have any money in the bank. I always just paid myself a set amount each month and handed a shoebox of receipts to my accountant at the end of the year.'

Oh dear!

Looking at the numbers he would have had to sell considerably more than £40,000 worth of plumbing services to return the same level of net profit in 2002 as he did in 2001. On our model, the sales figure he needs is £53,000 to make this level of profit, assuming that the cost of labour stays the same and that material costs are always half of the sales figure. In real life the actual number was closer to £80,000, and Steve gasped when I told him. It was almost double what he thought he needed to make enough money to keep going.

Inwardly I screamed a long, painful scream of frustration. This person could have run his business quite differently and made a profit. He could have taken some steps to protect himself against a sudden cash shortage, but his preference for shoeboxes and ignorance had laid him open and made him vulnerable, and now we were both going to pay the price.

'You do realize that you can't even afford to pay me for this session,' I observed, in a not unkind way. 'I'm happy to work for free today, but you really need to go and see your accountant and work out *exactly* what your financial position is, particularly your tax liabilities.'

'I will do that,' he replied, as if I had just asked him to go and buy an ice cream. He seemed not to have twigged that he was in the shit. The laptop had made it all look like some distant computer game. He continued, 'But first I would like some help to budget for next year. What should I do?'

Opposite is a partially completed copy of his P&L forecast for the next year, 2003. Using the 2001/2002 P&L from earlier and the notes underneath them, take a minute to write a budget for next year, by filling in the blanks. Can you make the net profit add up to £8,000? This was the number that Steve needed to keep trading. We can assume that he is capable of working at the same level as he did in 2001, and that he can ditch the extra staff and all the things he did to build up his business, which actually put it into reverse.

An answer is given on page 152 but don't turn to it until you have made an effort to complete the above. If you're wondering about the maths involved, gross profit is total sales less the cost of sales (materials and labour in this example) and net profit is gross profit less all overhead costs. The cost of labour has been set to nil because in a

Profit and Loss Account

	2003 Forecast	
	£	£
Sales	30,000	
Cost of materials	15,000	
Cost of labour	0	
Gross Profit		15,000
Overheads		
Office rent	?	
Heat & light	?	
Van hire	?	
Diesel	?	
Stationery	?	
Advertising	?	
Mobile phone	?	
Accountancy	?	
Bad debt	?	
Total Overhead		
Net Profit		

sole trader business like this one, Steve's wages come out of his net profit, after he has paid the costs of running his business.

The way to be successful is to be ruthless with costs and only ever spend what you have to. The more costs you incur, the harder you have to work just to stand still. It can feel like the right move to take on new people, or spend money on advertising, but if you don't have the revenue to cover it then you are eating into your profits.

Advertising can be a great way to bring in new business, but it can quickly drain your resources. Placing a single colour advert in a magazine can cost several hundred pounds, which could be the same as a whole year of going to networking meetings. A cheap way to advertise is to pay for leaflets to be inserted into your local paper. That can be an effective method of letting the local people know you exist, and it uses up all those extra leaflets you were talked into ordering, by some shiny-suited sales type.

Sitting with Steve, I realized that my hand-knitted PC-based spreadsheets were good enough to help me run my business because they had two important things going for them. Firstly, they were accurate – always a big plus point – and secondly, I understood how they were compiled. I only know the basics when it comes to using spreadsheets, and trying to make them do anything more complex than adding up a column of numbers generally gives me a headache. Every time I get a new sale, or before I decide to buy a piece of equipment, I type the numbers in and look at how the *net* profit changes. Then I always turn to a second spreadsheet which is linked and see what the impact is on the cashflow forecast.

Steve's cashflow forecast instantly told me that if he was a ship, it would be too late to launch the lifeboats. He was going down, unless he stopped buying things right now and worked out exactly how much money he had today and how much he already owed to people. I pointed this out to him, tactfully, and he stared at his computer screen for a moment. Then he agreed that he needed to bring his accounts up to date and needed to take some radical business decisions.

The wall of golfers broke up and the ladies started to drift home. Steve quietly packed up his laptop, shook my hand and headed off with them. Later that evening he emailed to say thank you for the session. It had opened his eyes to the severity of his situation, and although nervous, he was grateful.

The postscript to the story is that two years later he was investigated by the tax office, which refused to believe that his net profit could have declined that quickly. As a result he has had to dig out all his receipts going back several years to prove that he was not siphoning off money, which he wasn't. He might have been naïve, but he wasn't criminal.

Stop here, grab a sheet of squared paper and take some time to produce a profit and loss account for your business, showing the forecast results from your first three years of trading. In which month do you make your first small profit? What profit would you make if your assumptions were all correct? How much flexibility is there to earn less income than you predict? You won't truly know how accurate your forecasting is until after you have been trading for a full calendar year, when you will have a better idea of exactly what pops up each month. When you are satisfied you have a useful spreadsheet turn to your Personal Planning Kit, to section 16 called 'Lucky Numbers' (on page 177) and tick the box.

Having established the importance of making a profit, we need to finish with cashflow and the necessity of a cashflow forecast, which is to business what the little dial showing the remaining oxygen level is to an astronaut. Cash is the life blood of business, and most businesses that go bust don't do so because they make a loss. They go bust because they run out of cash, like a car tyre which runs flat after being ripped open by a shard of metal.

The reason for keeping this chapter to the end is because *cashflow* and *forecast* are two little words to have ringing in your ears once you have finished the book and placed it reverently back on your bookshelf, in its own little velvet-lined cubbyhole. If you do nothing else when you set up your business, then produce a cashflow forecast. Without it you are blind to the future, and having no cash is just no fun.

A cashflow forecast is there to help you plan your money. Do you need to borrow some? Do you need to spend less? Do you need to make sure your payment terms are 30 days and not 60 days? Do you need an extra revenue stream to make up for the income shortfall you expect in the summer holidays? All of these useful questions are there to be answered by the cashflow forecast.

A popular myth is that businesses are started to generate a profit. This is wrong, because profit without cash is a disaster.

The purpose of a business is to make a positive and increasing cashflow.

With cash you can buy stuff, you have power and in business terms you have strength and solidity.

One of the dangerous things that can happen to a business is called *over-trading*. The example that follows has been culled from a real-life decision made by a managing director who managed to ruin his business by winning a huge new order that was to be made from a special material. The order was a real coup for the business, and was worth several times the existing turnover (total sales). In one stunning jump the MD would transform the business and take it to dizzying new heights of success and wealth. What could be wrong with winning a great order? Isn't that what we all dream about? The story, as ever, is hidden in the numbers.

In this case the MD didn't ask his accountant to draw up a cashflow forecast, despite being urged to do so by a concerned friend. As the top man, the MD lived with the Gods and dined exclusively on nectar and ambrosia, which can be very filling. Have you ever seen a cherub in need of a square meal? He was senior to all those around him, and because his title automatically bestowed on him unassailable wisdom, nobody dared question his judgement.

Take a look at the example cashflow forecast overleaf, and look for clues as to what went wrong. Start by looking at the opening and closing bank balances, and then notice what happens in the business in July and August. The numbers are to scale and have been simplified to make them quicker to read.

What have you noticed? What is the story here? The order should have generated an extra £30,000 of cash from the opening position at the start of May, but in reality it didn't. If this was your business, what would you have done before August if you knew your cash was all going to be sucked out so quickly?

The business was doing pretty well until the MD's mega-order hit the shop floor. The material arrived for it in July and had to be paid for right away, which drained cash out of the business. Most of the workers were now involved in making the special items to be shipped, and as a result only a few people were left to complete existing orders from the regular customers who had sustained the business for many years. However, the wages and the overhead costs still had to be paid each month, and these took more bites out of the cash reserves the business had.

Because considerably fewer orders shipped to customers during July and August, the cash income was reduced 30 days later in August (from July sales) and in September (from August sales). In theory, the big order should have despatched in September to be paid in October and all would have been well. In real life it never left the factory.

The 'Problem of Over-Trading' Example

Item	May	June	July	Aug	Sept	Oct
Opening Cash at the bank	50	50	40	10	(20)	(50)
Plus cash due in from sales	100	80	100	40	40	200
Less material costs to be paid	50	40	80	20	20	20
Less wages to be paid	40	40	40	40	40	40
Less overhead costs to be paid	10	10	10	10	10	10
Closing Cash at the bank	50	40	10	(20)	(50)	80
			Special material arrives		Special order to ship	

Notes:
The numbers are all £000, so '50' means £50,000.
Numbers in brackets like (20) are negative numbers, which indicates the business owes the bank money.

The timescale to completion slipped, as the workers struggled to make their existing machines deal with the new material. They were also overwhelmed by the sheer size of the order, which their systems and working practices were not designed to cope with. The order did not leave the factory in September or October, or even November, but cash to pay for materials, wages and overheads still had to be found. Eventually the business ran over its overdraft limit, ran out of folding money, ran out of small change, ran over its own feet and then stopped dead.

The MD stood stoically in front of the workforce and said that nothing could be done. The business had gone into receivership and they were all out of a job. Yesterday they had been working hard and today they were hard at work looking for new jobs. The MD was asked what went wrong. He thought about it and told the workers that it was because of the recession and that nothing could have been done. It was out of his hands. The bastard!

This true and sad story shows what happens when a business over-trades. When it takes too long to complete work and fails to earn enough money in the meantime to pay the bills, it goes to the wall and gets sprayed with graffiti. The saddest part of all, in this case, was that it was totally avoidable, and a good business was ruined through the ignorance of one moronic and arrogant Managing Director.

If you are tempted by a juicy order that will stretch your resources, there are some simple steps to take to avoid running out of cash. They include these four top picks:

1 Produce a cashflow forecast and discuss the implications with your accountant or bank manager. If you have to borrow money, think about the cost of doing so.
2 Be prepared to subcontract work to increase capacity and to keep existing customers happy, so that they continue to bring cash into the business.
3 Ask for stage payments from the customer of the big order to offset the cost of buying materials. This is common in the building industry where there can be long lead times to project completion.
4 Don't accept the order. You can walk away and instead of taking big bites out of the market place, nibble away at it. Just like eating, it's difficult to swallow when your mouth is crammed with food. Take smaller bites and swallow more comfortably.

The last point is perhaps the one that can be the hardest to do. When you have worked hard to grow your business it can seem insane to turn work away. I have turned down a number of contracts because I just didn't have the capacity to do them. On paper I could have shuffled things around, but it would have meant such a punishing workload that I was in danger of succumbing to exhaustion.

A sales manager I knew turned down the chance to tender for a lucrative contract, and when the operations director returned from his holiday and found out about the decision he went berserk and ranted at the unfortunate manager for some time. Eventually his ire burnt itself out and my friend was able to show him the implications for the factory if the tender had been won. The director was instantly apologetic, as he realized that far from being lazy in refusing to bid for the contract, the manager had in fact narrowly avoided a disaster.

Finance may not be everyone's idea of fun. If it was then the world would be full of accountants, and what a weird place that would be. However, businesses and money are inseparable. The key point to draw out of the examples of profit and loss and cashflow is that *you* are *responsible* for knowing about your business.

A hairdresser friend of mine does her books every single day as soon as she gets home, so that she remains on top of her finances. She knows that if she slips behind she is unable to make decisions based on current information, and this could harm her salon – a salon that has been run very successfully for many years, on the back of accurate and current financial information. And sharp scissors, of course.

Simple spreadsheets can be very effective, but like all such tools they need to be constantly updated, or they're junk.

If your business doesn't seem to be able to make a profit, trim back your expenses and be ruthless with costs. If your cashflow forecast shows less money at the end of the year than at the beginning, then you have a problem, which needs to be fixed. Play with the numbers if it helps, but remember to be cautious with guesses.

Now, before we potter off to read the final chapter, here

> Turn to your Personal Planning Kit for the last time and complete section 17, called 'Cash or Crash' (on page 178). Well done for completing the kit, and remember to keep it in a safe place.

is my answer to the P&L question about budgeting for Steve for 2003. I have based my answers on the notes under the 2001 and 2002 spreadsheet. Did your forecast make as much money as possible, or did you stick to just answering the question? It proves the point that you can always squeeze the costs hard to help yourself to some easy profit. Or to put it another way, your profit is proportional to your ruthlessness with costs.

If you made £8,000 or more, then well done. If you didn't, take a look at your own business budgeting. Ask yourself if you are really being hard on costs, or are your sales forecast figures flabby guesses with no more chance of achieving sustainable flight than an elephant with a hang-glider? You really don't want to get a spanking, do you?

That's the hard bit out of the way: two salutary stories to illustrate the need to have a freshly brewed profit and loss spreadsheet and a cashflow forecast in your tea pots of business professionalism. Without them we would all be playing at business, in the same way kids play with conkers. They take a coupe of swipes and then get really cross when their ten-winner-bomber gets smashed up by the kid with glasses wielding a double-baked vinegar-soaked interconti-nental ballistic conker. And when he wins, by blasting your prize specimen to chaff, you are too surprised to remove his glasses and slap him. Business is the same and it's often the kids with glasses who turn out to do rather well. Not

Steve the Plumber
Profit and Loss Account

	2003 forecast	
	£	£
Sales	30,000	
Cost of materials	15,000	
Cost of labour	0	
Gross profit		15,000
Overheads		
Office rent	500	
Heat & light	250	
Van hire	1,500	
Diesel	1,000	
Stationery	250	
Advertising	500	
Mobile phone	500	
Accountancy	500	
Bad debt	1,000	
Total Overhead		6,000
Net Profit		9,000

because they are strong and tough, but because they are thoughtful and make sure they have all their business conkers well soaked and ready to go out and win for them.

Now that the world of numbers is behind us, we have almost reached the end of the book, where we can celebrate how far we've come and then head off into the world. Switch off your brain for a moment, or push the button that drops it into sleep mode, sit back and relax. Rest your feet on the cat and breathe deeply.

It's time to pull on our flares, flowered shirts and bangles. It's time to feel groovy, man.

Love is Groovy

Celebrate your baby business

12

I love my little business. It has bits of me sewn into the lining, and it's been cut and patched like the sleeves of my favourite cardigan. What started out as a way of having a fulfilling working life has become something more than 'just a job'. It's a bit like the greasy teenager who buys an old car and then keeps adding spoilers, fancy paint, fog lights and subwoofers that are so powerful they create a small earthquake if they are cranked beyond '5' on the volume scale. On one level the car is still just an average little runabout. On another it's a stripped-out, pimped-up passion wagon which has the owner's DNA encoded on the re-chipped engine management system.

To me, my business is a low-slung, street-burning customer-catcher with the power to slay the competition, if I choose to unleash the thermonuclear networking capability and trigger the heat-seeking leaflet dispensers with radar guided database targeting. My business is so sleek and sexy that it purrs. If it were a tiger, it would be the sort of beast which slips into a London nightclub and spends a happy night flicking fivers at the topless tigress on stage, just for the hell of it, while sipping exotically titled cocktails: Sex on a Beach, Humping in a Hammock and Pussy by a Pool, to name but three. As I said, I love my business.

The trouble is that I'm the only one who has this libidinous attachment. A man may spend hours in a cold garage, lovingly breathing life into his rusty old traction engine, but to his mates and his family he's as mad as a box of beavers.

I'm happy to be mad. I've only got the one life, so I may as well follow my heart.

I enjoy what I do. I have learned the hard way how to sell, how to market myself and how to network. My contracting has sharpened up and my assumptions have been trimmed back to reality. I enjoy meeting new people and I keep on top of my accounts each month.

Sometimes I still make mistakes, like the day when my wife returned home to find a huge silver car parked on the drive and a very cross consultant sitting in it.

'What are you doing here?' asked my bemused wife, whilst wrangling two small and interested children.

'I have a sales meeting with Richard,' he replied through gritted teeth. 'He's late.'

'No, he's not. He's away on business,' she replied.

The man left in a huff, and I had to make a very uncomfortable telephone call to him to apologize for my poor diary keeping. The episode crimped that particular happy day, and ever since I have been meticulous in keeping my diary free of scribbles and crossings out, which were to blame for the confusion.

However, despite these odd hiccups I know that I am *good enough*, and that all I need to do is to keep on being good enough to survive. Perfection is a useless concept, and one that can really get in the way, so if you're tempted to reach for it, stop now, grab your jacket and go down to the pub for a game of pool and a slice of real life.

When I am away from home seeing clients, my chair stays empty. Sometimes I can be found sitting in my car with a smug smile on my face because I know that it will never be filled in my absence by a manager who rummages through my desk looking for incriminating evidence, or an unexpected replacement who chucks out my pen tidy and swaps the photos of my gorgeous kids for his ugly brood.

I smile too, that I have not had a crappy appraisal this year and have not been set a bunch of stupid objectives which are expected to 'help' me develop. My subconscious is very happy with my performance and has awarded me several small treats and the occasional pay rise. I even took an afternoon off last year! How cool is that!

Working for yourself is work. It is a real job. People who work for themselves often say, 'When I had a proper job ....' Tut tut tut, that's no good. Saying that just undermines what you are doing. Be proud of your decisions and your achievements. Puff out your chest with pride. Whatever you choose to do, whichever path you take when you leave the bastards behind, love your business and it will love you back. That's the final secret of working for yourself.

Love your business.

Hug it and keep it warm, and it will grow and you will be successful. Wrap it in a blanket sometimes and feed it on a diet of quality customers, who all pay high prices and who all pay on time. Have fun with your life, and remember that you can be a great success in your chosen field.

If you are wondering:

Should I?

Could I?

Dare I?

Then if you have read this far, the answer is probably 'yes'. You *can*. You can do it. You can choose for yourself. Life and success and happiness is all about choice. It always is.

Have fun with your choices.

Thank you for reading this.

Go well and goodbye.

Personal Planning Kit

Cut out and keep safe

Every business is run by different people and so is different in some aspects. The same is true for the planning needed to start up. Examples of more traditional business plans can be had for free from most major banks and building societies, and this personal planning kit is here to provide people with the basic building blocks.

Because of the variation in size, scope and the needs of new businesses, the personal planning kit is not intended to be exhaustive, or it would run to several hundred pages. Instead it is there to bite off big chunks of thinking and to focus you on answering some of those thorny questions which will have to be addressed if you are to be a successful selfer. Remember though, that you are responsible for the choices you make and the actions or inactions you decide upon as a result of completing it.

We generously offer you a no-quibble, no-guarantee contract here that says, with a warm smile on our face, good luck and you're on your own.

Remember not to get *spanked*!

Have fun!

Personal Planning Kit

This Personal Planning Kit belongs to:

_____

Date of completion: _____

Compass points to guide you

- Simplicity is your greatest asset.
- Spend nothing until you need to.
- Keep you hands and your money in your pockets.
- Do what you can for free.
- Update your cashflow forecast each week.
- You are your business.
- Remember to watch out for fireworks.
- Love your business and it will love you back.

Avoid a spanking

S **Self** – check out your own awareness and your style of working.
P **Plan** – cash, time, budgets, networking.
A **Assumptions** – you will live or die by them.
N **Networking** – tell people you exist.
K **Kick ass** – Get going: business requires energy, motivation and slog.

To download a copy of your Personal Planning Kit, please visit **www.richardmaun.com**

Section 1: A Sense of the Future (page 14)

Part A: Relax and let your thoughts and feelings swill about. What is your sense of what you would like to do? No need to be precise, if you're not too sure. Write down the *sort* of thing that you fancy having a go at:

_____

_____

_____

_____

_____

_____

Part B: Now imagine you are doing some of the stuff from Part A. For fun, have a go at describing what your working week, or an average day, looks like. Write it, draw it or just jot down some points to capture the feeling of actually being there:

_____

_____

_____

_____

_____

_____

Part C: What new skills or experience do you need to acquire to help turn your dream into a reality? How will you get what you need?

_____

_____

_____

_____

_____

_____

Part D: What resources will your business need to get started? Think about equipment, people, premises, stock, insurance, training and any critical 'must have' items:

_____

_____

_____

_____

_____

_____

_____

_____

Part E: What type of business will you be? Tick an option:

- ❏ Sole trader

- ❏ Limited company

- ❏ Partnership

Section 2: Assumptions and Bank of Family (page 23)

Part A: **Assumptions.** List the ones you are making about the size and shape of your business – and remember to look around you at current competitors. If your local florist drives an old van, then wonder why. Or if your chum who is a consultant spends all her time away from home, ask her how much she spends on food and hotels ...

_____

_____

_____

_____

_____

_____

_____

Part B: **Bank of Family.** How much emotional credit do you have lodged with them, that you can draw on to support you through the tough times ahead? On a scale of 1 to 50 ask *your family* to put a cross on the line to show you where they are:

1--50
(not much credit)   (loads of credit)

Section 3: The Fireworks Code (page 42)

Copy your scores onto the scales and then circle the firework that best represents the behaviour others are likely to see from you:

A Thinking

Quick,
or shallow   – 1 2 3 4 5 6 7 8 9 10 –   Deep thinking,
thinking   or fixated
                                                                       thinking

B Activity

Inactivity,   Train-track
or sluggish   – 1 2 3 4 5 6 7 8 9 10 –   direction, or
movement   shotgun approach

Firework Model of Stress (FMoS)		
Hyper Thinking	Catherine Wheel Round in circles	Rocket Lost in space
Lazy Thinking	Damp squib Fizzle out...	Fountain Shotgun Approach
BEHAVIOUR	**Lazy Activity**	**Hyper Activity**

Section 4: Your Supporters Club (page 46)

Note down the contact details and the reason why each person is on your list. If you're stuck for a great reason, then choose again:

1 _____
_____
_____
_____
_____

2 _____
_____
_____
_____
_____

3 _____
_____
_____
_____
_____

4 _____
_____
_____
_____
_____

5 _____
_____
_____
_____

6

7

8

9

10

Section 5: Team Questions (page 48)

Add five more questions to the list that you would like to ask your supporters club. Any question that has value to you is a good question! Useful questions:

1 What questions do I need to ask you?
2 If you were starting today, what would you do differently?
3 How do you find new customers?
4 When did you get it wrong and what did you learn?
5 Who do you know who would be useful for me to talk to?

6 _____

7 _____

8 _____

9 _____

10 _____

Section 6: I am Special Because ... (page 50)

Write down the strengths, skills and useful experiences you have which you would share with clients, in order for them to be reassured that you are worth spending money with:

1 My strengths include:

_____

_____

_____

_____

_____

_____

_____

2 My skills include:

_____

_____

_____

_____

_____

_____

3 My relevant experience includes:

_____

_____

_____

_____

_____

_____

Section 7: Creating an Opening (page 62)

Ask questions to get the client talking and to generate an opening, which you can fill with your product and/or service. Note three examples, one closed and two open:

Closed question:

_____

_____

_____

_____

_____

_____?

Open question:

_____

_____

_____

_____

_____

_____?

Open question:

_____

_____

_____

_____

_____

_____?

Section 8: Selling by Numbers (page 69)

List the products you will sell, the volume of your sales in the first year and the price you will sell them for. Then add up your guesses, trim them back to 80 per cent and discover whether this income will pay all the bills. An example is included – and remember to leave it out of your totals!

Item	Volume per year	Unit price	Volume x price = sales	Be cautious	Cautious total
Cheese roll	5,000	£0.75	£3,750	x 80% =	£3,000
Total forecast	=				

Section 9: The Name Game (page 78)

My three possible business names are:

1_____

2_____

3_____

Tick when you have checked them at Companies House, the Patent Office and made sure the website address is available for your favourite: ☐

Section 10: Differentiate or Die (page 82)

Part A: Write down the negative messages you have in your head, then cross them out! They no longer have value to you:

_____

_____

_____

_____

_____

Part B: Write down what you know about your closest competitor. What products/services does he/she/it offer? Why do people buy from them?

_____

_____

_____

_____

_____

Part C: Yourself. What do you well?

_____

_____

_____

_____

_____

Part D: Your business. Think about what you will do. How will you do it differently from your competitor? Remember to include small details, as all differences have value.

_____

_____

_____

_____

_____

Section 11: Marketing Toolbox (page 85)

Which marketing tools will you need to let people know you exist? Tick the ones you will organize, but think about the costs involved as well, as you may not need or be able to afford all of them.

❑ Business card

❑ Pre-printed letterhead

❑ Compliments slip

❑ One-page leaflet

❑ Multi-page brochure

❑ Press release

❑ Magazine advert

❑ Special packaging

Section 12: Net·Work (page 95)

What specific business opportunity will you be asking the people in your network to look out for? Write it here in one short sentence.

☺ I am looking for:

_____

_____

_____

_____

_____

_____

_____

Secondly, think about people you already know to whom you could mention this opportunity. Add as many names as you can to each of the categories below:

☺ Friends

☺ Family

☺ Leisure clubs

☺ Ex-colleagues

☺ Suppliers

☺ Competitors

☺ Local businesses

☺ Who else?

Section 13: Your Skinny Minute (page 102)

Write down eight key points that describe your business.
Paula's Pets is used as an example on the right-hand side.

Your business	Paula's Pets
1.	1. Exotic
2.	2. Reptiles
3.	3. Five years
4.	4. Homes and schools
5.	5. Seven poisonous snakes
6.	6. Insurance
7.	7. Pole dancing
8.	8. Chameleons

Section 14: Trawling (page 114)

Clear contracting for success is about the administrative details, the goals and processes and the fishy bits. Write down three questions Peter could have asked at his interview to find some of the fish which were clearly lurking in the depths:

Q1 _____

_____

_____

_____

_____

_____

_____ ?

Q2 _____

_____

_____

_____

_____

_____

_____ ?

Q3 _____

_____

_____

_____

_____

_____

_____ ?

Section 15: The Height Chart (page 130)

Tick the box that best describes your mood today, then cement this by colouring in the cartoon on top of the bar of your current stage.

- ☐ **Baby** – just born into an exciting world
- ☐ **Toddler** – one or two skills, lots of enthusiasm
- ☐ **Teenager** – fed up and worried at your lack of instant success
- ☐ **Middle Ager** – worldly and experienced, some success balanced by continued effort
- ☐ **Old Codger** – sustainable and complacent, watch out for the younger hungry types

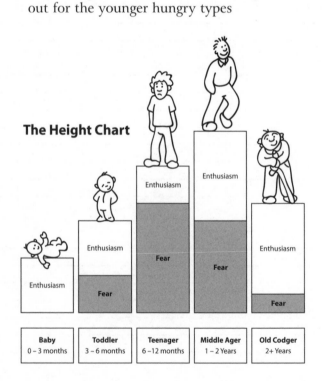

Section 16: Lucky Numbers (page 145)

Produce a profit and loss spreadsheet for your first three years of trading. Use the example in the chapter as a guide if it helps. Then when you have a useful document, tick the box!

❑ I have a P&L spreadsheet that I am happy with ☺

Section 17: Cash or Crash (page 151)

If you do nothing else by way of business planning, at least draw up a cashflow forecast. Check your assumptions and build in some contingency, because it will rain at some point! Then tick the boxes:

❑ I have a cashflow forecast covering the first six months.

❑ I have a cashflow forecast covering the first two years, taking me into a successful position.

☺ Celebration Time

Well done me, for making it this far. I have completed a useful planning exercise and feel very proud of myself. Full of confidence, I can tick 'yes' to the following essential skills and resources:

❏ I have talent.

❏ I will be successful.

❏ I understand the difference between profit and cash.

❏ I know what sort of firework best describes me.

❏ I have a sexy skinny minute in my pocket.

❏ I am ready to work my network.

❏ I am a special loveable person who can follow their own path in life.

❏ I have my own chair and I'm keeping it to myself!

Hooray!

The bastards are now way behind me and the future looks fantastic.

About the Author

Richard Maun is a professional business manager who has worked in industry for many years. He now enjoys life as a freelance business writer, as a director of his own company and as a visiting lecturer to a leading UK university. Richard facilitates personal and business development through coaching, management consultancy and interactive workshops, and he specializes in personal communication skills. He has worked with a wide variety of people to help them act in awareness, develop new thinking, turn conflict into collaboration and learn about themselves in a safe and supportive way.

Richard Maun can be contacted at:
www.richardmaun.com